# Going G

## Piers Connor

Capital Transport

First published 1993
Second edition 1994

ISBN 185414 162 7

Published in association with the District Line, London Underground Ltd,
by Capital Transport Publishing, 38 Long Elmes, Harrow Weald, Middlesex

Printed by The KPC Group, Ashford, Kent

© Piers Connor 1993

The author and publisher would like to thank Nick Agnew, Desmond F. Croome,
Mike Horne and Alan A. Jackson for assistance with the preparation of this book.

The front cover painting is by Peter Green, GRA

The back cover poster and the other posters in this book
are copyright London Transport Museum

CONTENTS

**Early District – Earl's Court about 1878.** LT Museum U13786

# The Beginnings of the District

The first section of the District Line, between South Kensington and Westminster, was opened on 24th December 1868. Its origins can be found five years earlier, just after the opening on 10th January 1863 of the Metropolitan Railway along what is now the northern section of the Circle Line between Paddington and Farringdon.

The Metropolitan Railway had been born as a result of a long perceived need for a railway to connect the City of London with both the main line railway termini at King's Cross, Euston and Paddington and with what were then the outskirts of the built up area of London. The railway was backed by business interests and property owners in the City who regarded it principally as a means of encouraging the working classes of the inner city area to move further out to obtain better accommodation and thus release land for commercial exploitation. As the area along the route was densely built up, it was decided to build the railway underground, even though, apart from horses, steam was the only reliable means of traction in those days.

In spite of its smoky atmosphere, the Metropolitan was a success. This and the growing need to provide rail links for the considerable traffic moving between other main line railway termini in London, led to a proposal from a House of Lords select committee for an 'inner circuit' railway which would connect both ends of the Metropolitan's line in a loop via the south side of the City. In conjunction with this scheme, which we now know as the Circle Line, it was proposed to incorporate a new road running along the north bank of the Thames called the Embankment. This new road had been proposed from time to time over the previous thirty years and the opportunity was taken to incorporate it in plans for the inner circuit railway to help with its financing.

It was considered that the Metropolitan Railway was not capable on its own of raising sufficient capital, nor of managing the very large construction project needed to complete the Circle Line. A second company was therefore formed, known as the Metropolitan District Railway, later to become popularly known as the District Railway. The purpose of this company was to raise capital and construct the railway along the south side of the Circle while the Metropolitan completed the north side. It was intended that eventually the two companies would merge as soon as it was financially possible. The Circle was to include single connections with the main line railways at Farringdon and Liverpool Street and a double connection with the West London Extension Railway northwards towards Addison Road (now Olympia) and southwards at West Brompton. These were to connect with the Circle alignment at High Street Kensington and Gloucester Road.

**Gloucester Road station nearing completion in 1868.** LT Museum

Under an agreement made in 1866, the trains on the initial section of the District were operated by the Metropolitan Railway (which had reached Gloucester Road from Paddington on 1st October 1868) and were effectively an extension of that company's service from what was to become the north side of the Circle Line. Completion of this first section, from South Kensington to Westminster Bridge, on 24th December 1868 had been pushed forward in an attempt to maximise revenue — Christmas traffic on the railways was then much heavier than it is today. There were intermediate stations at Sloane Square, Victoria and St James's Park.

The second section of the District to open was the link between the District side of Gloucester Road station and West Brompton, which was covered by a Metropolitan Railway shuttle service from 12th April 1869. Junctions had been made with the Metropolitan Railway tracks at Gloucester Road and the curve from what was later Earl's Court to High Street Kensington and the link between Earl's Court and the West London Railway were also ready, although not yet in use for public services. No permanent connection was made at this time, or subsequently, to the West London Extension Railway at West Brompton. The northern curve to the West London Railway was first used regularly from 1st February 1872, when the LNWR started its 'Outer Circle' service between Broad Street and Mansion House via Willesden Junction.

**South Kensington station in the 1890s. The Metropolitan bay platform is on the right.**

Construction eastwards along the new river embankment proved a difficult engineering task, exacerbated by financial problems, but the 1⅓-mile extension to Blackfriars was finally opened on 30th May 1870, with intermediate stations at Charing Cross (now Embankment) and Temple. Again the Metropolitan Railway extended its existing service.

At the western end, between Gloucester Road and east of South Kensington station, a second pair of tracks was provided for the District, parallel to the Metropolitan tracks, and each company was to have its own platforms at these two stations with a separate ticket office to collect its own fares. The District tracks were on the southern side and came into use on 1st August 1870 when a District service, worked by the Metropolitan, began to ply between West Brompton and Blackfriars. However the District side of South Kensington station was not completed until July 1871, when the flat junction between the two sets of tracks was moved from the west to the east side of the station.

Around the middle of 1869, arguments began to simmer between the Metropolitan and the District; the older company used the terms of the 1866 agreement to impose a surcharge which reduced the District's net income by 38%, whilst the District pressed for more frequent services to increase its revenue, perceived to be less than that of

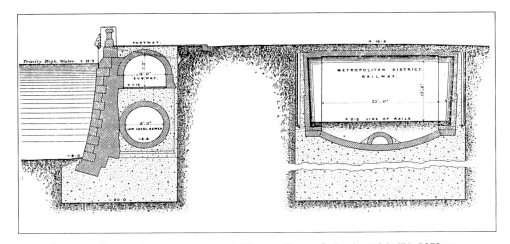

A cross section showing the arrangement of the new Thames Embankment, built in 1870 as a combined project with the construction of the District Railway between Westminster and Blackfriars. The railway and road opened within six weeks of each other, on 30th May and 13th July 1870 respectively.

Opposite **Original District Railway locomotive with four-coach train at West Brompton in 1876, probably bound for High Street Kensington.** LT Museum

the Metropolitan on its own lines. The aggrieved District sought the advice of James Staats Forbes, combative general manager of the London, Chatham and Dover Railway, who at once began to encourage moves towards independence from the Metropolitan. Forbes became a District director in October 1870. In 1871, following the resignation of the Metropolitan representatives on the District board, he assumed the office of managing director, becoming chairman and managing director in November 1872.

Forbes' influence firmly diverted the District board on to the path of complete separation from the Metropolitan Railway, which was now under notice that the District wished to terminate from July 1871 the working agreement made in 1866. Thus the original intention for unified management of London's planned Inner Circle service was doomed and much quarrelling over it was to ensue.

Another cause of friction was the construction by the District, without parliamentary authority or the agreement of the Metropolitan, of what became known as the 'Cromwell Curve', two tracks parallel to the Metropolitan's affording a direct run for the MDR over its own line, between Gloucester Road and High Street Kensington. This link, completed in July 1870, was seen by the Metropolitan as a means for the District to reduce its mileage (and thus its costs) over the jointly-worked Inner Circle and of increasing its receipts by diverting its trains over its own line west of South Kensington. The Curve was used briefly in the summer of 1871 for a West Brompton – High Street (reverse) – Mansion House service. Although the boundaries between the two companies in this area were settled by arbitration in 1871, arguments about the use of Curve continued for over 30 years until the matter was taken to court in 1903. The Metropolitan then won the right to use it, although this right was rarely exercised.

Forbes was able to help the District secure its own trains by arranging hire purchase. Locomotives were ordered in December 1870, coaches a month later and all were delivered in time for the extension further east to Mansion House station on 3rd July 1871. To house and maintain its new trains, the District built a depot and workshops at what was to become known as Lillie Bridge, just west of the curve from Earl's Court to the West London Railway. These buildings had concrete walls, interesting in that the District was something of a pioneer in the use of this material. The depot was reached by a single line connection to the West London Railway curve, an arrangement which required all trains entering or leaving it to reverse. Lillie Bridge was not finished until the summer of 1872.

Concurrently with the opening to Mansion House (3rd July 1871), the District platforms at High Street Kensington and South Kensington came into public use, together with the curve from Earl's Court to High Street. In addition to joint operation with the Metropolitan of what was to become the Inner Circle, the District also worked its own trains between West Brompton and High Street.

Much valuable experience was gained during the construction of the Metropolitan Railway and this was used in the planning of the District. Originally, to reduce the smoke from the trains in the tunnels, it was intended to use fireless locomotives in which the steam would be generated by water heated from fire bricks. Experiments with a trial locomotive designed this way were conducted in 1862 but it failed to provide the power required to haul trains.

It was therefore decided that conventional locomotives would be used but that these would have their exhaust steam condensed in their side tanks when running through the tunnel. This did not prevent serious pollution of the tunnel atmosphere along the Metropolitan's original section and alterations had to be made later to provide openings at intervals along the line. When designing the Metropolitan's extensions round its part of the Circle and the line for the District, Mr Fowler, originally the Chief Engineer to both companies, arranged for the stations to be in the open as much as possible and provided cuttings at each end of the platforms and at intermediate points along the route.

Between Gloucester Road and Mansion House the line was constructed by the cut and cover method. This involved digging a deep cutting along the line of route which was then roofed over where necessary, usually by brick arches. The difficulty with this method of construction was that it caused a great deal of surface disruption. Once the disruption along the route of the original Metropolitan railway had been seen, owners of properties all over London fought vigorously against the introduction of an underground railway in their area. The 'not in my back yard' brigade were just as forceful in Victorian times as they are today. More so in those days perhaps, because they were afraid of damage to their property in addition to the disruption of their lives during construction. They also did not want to be living near a railway which ran underground and was powered by steam.

The route was built to a standard width of 25ft, wide enough for two tracks. Double-width cuttings of 50ft were provided for stations. Platforms were usually 15ft wide and about 300ft long. They were wooden until they were rebuilt for the electrification of the line in 1905.

Stations were provided with glazed, arched roofs built with wrought iron frames. None of the original roofs remain on the District but good examples have survived at the former Metropolitan stations at Notting Hill Gate and Paddington. The original roof at West Brompton has survived but it seems to have been an experiment, as it was angled rather than arched and could be said to be the prototype for similar roofs built in the late 1870s at Earl's Court and Ealing Broadway.

When the line was first opened through to West Brompton there was no station at Earl's Court. The site was in the middle of market garden land and there were few houses in the area. However, sufficient land was taken for four tracks as the original plans stipulated separate pairs of lines between High Street Kensington and Addison Road and between West Brompton and Gloucester Road. Once the line opened, local residents petitioned for a station. It was built with a small wooden booking office on the east side of Earl's Court Road and two platforms serving three tracks and opened on 31st October 1871. It lasted only until 1875 when, on 30th December, it was destroyed by fire.

During the four years from the opening of Earl's Court station, the surrounding area had been rapidly built up. The coming of the railway made it an attractive place to live whilst working in the City, a development pattern to be followed throughout the Greater London area over the next 100 years. The opportunity was taken to provide a larger station, and a new site to the west of the old was chosen. The area was widened and the present day station with its overall roof was built. Work began in 1876 and the station was opened to the public on 1st February 1878. At the same time, the layout at the east end of the station was eased by building a flyunder for the westbound line from High Street Kensington which passed under the main line from Gloucester Road.

At St James's Park station a short tunnel was built at the east end on the north side which housed a locomotive lay-by and was connected to the eastbound track. It was closed when the line opened to Mansion House and was subsequently used as a store.

**A gas lit Earl's Court station before electrification. The general appearance of the station is little changed today apart from the stairwells for the Piccadilly Line platforms below and the clutter of kiosks.** LT Museum H10948

Further sidings were provided at Charing Cross (now Embankment). One connected with the eastbound track just east of the platform while the other connected with the westbound track just west of the station. Years later the sidings were removed and when the platforms were lengthened they were extended into the spaces thus vacated. This accounts for the fact that the platforms are not now directly opposite each other.

The station at Mansion House had three tracks with two platforms. A siding with coal and water facilities was provided on each side of the main tracks at the western end of the station. At the eastern end a concourse was placed under a five-storey building which housed the booking hall, above which was a restaurant, one of a chain operated by Spiers and Pond. The remaining floors provided living quarters for the restaurant staff. In later years, the Chairman of Spiers & Pond Ltd, Paul Cremieu-Javal, became involved in the exhibitions (of which more later) which were to provide so much traffic for the District over the years.

# The District Looks West

The opening of the lines to Mansion House, High Street Kensington, Addison Road and West Brompton marked the completion of the works authorised by the District's original Act of incorporation dated 29th July 1864, some eight years earlier. Although it had been expected that traffic levels would match those of the Metropolitan on the north side of the city, they were comparatively light, perhaps due to the variety of main line termini, any of which could be reached easily from south London and which removed the need to travel between them once reaching London.

The huge expense of building its line and the disappointing traffic levels had left the District in a vulnerable position. Its break with the Metropolitan in the belief that it was better off without it left it exposed to a hostile takeover. This possibility was emphasised by the appointment of Sir Edward Watkin as Chairman of the Metropolitan in 1872. Watkin was Chairman of the South Eastern Railway and deadly rival of the competing London Chatham & Dover and District director James Forbes. Forbes had long recognised the need to expand the District to draw in traffic, increase its income and consolidate its position. It had to get to the larger traffic centres and, to this end, looked towards Hammersmith, Kew and Richmond.

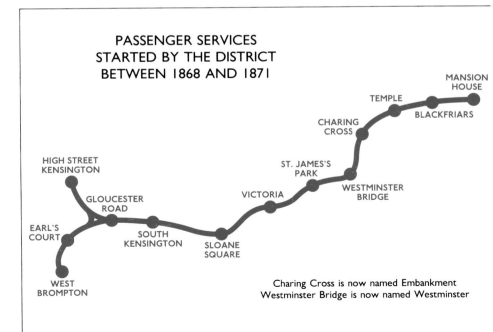

PASSENGER SERVICES
STARTED BY THE DISTRICT
BETWEEN 1868 AND 1871

MANSION HOUSE

TEMPLE

BLACKFRIARS

CHARING CROSS

HIGH STREET KENSINGTON

ST. JAMES'S PARK

VICTORIA

WESTMINSTER BRIDGE

GLOUCESTER ROAD

EARL'S COURT

SOUTH KENSINGTON

SLOANE SQUARE

WEST BROMPTON

Charing Cross is now named Embankment
Westminster Bridge is now named Westminster

Until the 1870s, most of the land west of Kensington was open country with a few villages and small towns. Compared with the expense of tunnelling, building lines across this land would be relatively cheap. In 1872, the District proposed an extension from Earl's Court to Barnes where it would connect with the London & South Western Railway and give it access to Kew and Richmond. However, this missed the significant traffic centre of Hammersmith, which was already served by the Hammersmith & City line jointly owned by the Metropolitan and the Great Western Railways. It was also served by an LSWR line, which ran between the West London Railway at Addison Road and Richmond and passed through the western edge of the town. In spite of this and the fact that it had a huge capital debt and was very short on credit, the District decided to push for a Hammersmith extension. It did so by the device of setting up a separate company to obtain capital. This was authorised under an Act of 1873 and the line opened to passenger traffic on 9th September 1874.

The new line started at a junction with the District's route to Addison Road at the end of the tunnel under the West London Extension Railway and then had to pass under the depot at Lillie Bridge. The rest of the line was in the open. One intermediate station was built at West Kensington. Barons Court station did not appear until 9th October 1905. The new line also gave another route into Lillie Bridge Depot from the eastbound Hammersmith line just east of West Kensington.

The District was now so close to the LSWR Addison Road to Richmond line that it became a much cheaper proposition to construct a connection to it than build the Barnes route. An agreement was reached with the LSWR that allowed the District to work over the LSWR line between Hammersmith and Richmond on condition it abandoned the Barnes proposal. Another District extension company (called the Metropolitan District Richmond Extension Railway) was therefore formed to build a short line from Hammersmith station to a junction with the LSWR line at Studland Road Junction, just east of Shaftesbury Road station (renamed Ravenscourt Park in 1888). It was authorised in 1875 and opened to traffic on 1st June 1877.

The District station at Hammersmith was originally designed as a terminus but, within two years of its opening in 1874, work began on its widening to accommodate the additional tracks for the Richmond extension. A new layout emerged with two terminal tracks on the north side and three through tracks on the south side. Hammersmith station was completely destroyed by fire on 20th January 1882 and it took seven months to rebuild.

District trains began working between Mansion House and Richmond from 1st June 1877. Trains from the Midland Railway also appeared as a result of an agreement to allow them to run off the LSWR's Richmond line to High Street Kensington and South Kensington. They never worked to South Kensington but built a coal depot next to Lillie Bridge depot at West Kensington, gaining access to it from a junction at the west end of the station. They built another coal depot at High Street Kensington. Both were opened in 1878. The Midland only exercised their rights to operate passenger services by running trains from St Pancras via Childs Hill, Willesden, Acton Lane Junction and the LSWR lines to Hammersmith and Earl's Court until September 1880 but coal train services continued into BR days and were finally withdrawn in July 1965.

With Turnham Green getting a better connection to the City of London the developers soon moved in. London's first Garden Suburb was started at Bedford Park close to Turnham Green station. Many of the houses were designed in the Queen Anne style and were intended for the better off. Rents were upwards from £40 per year, a high level for those days.

The opening of the District to Hammersmith had been quickly followed by a rapid increase in housing development all along the line between there and Gloucester Road. This encouraged the District to build further extensions so that, even while the Richmond extension works were in hand at Hammersmith, plans for an extension to Ealing were being prepared. The policy of extending into rural areas ripe for development was fuelled by a desire to generate traffic to help pay for the debt incurred by the expensive construction of the Gloucester Road to Mansion House section.

The Ealing extension was proposed with the express purpose of getting a connection with the Great Western Railway at Ealing Broadway and projecting District services to Windsor and Uxbridge. The route as far as Turnham Green was to be over the LSWR Richmond line with the new line being built by the District over the next 2½ miles to Ealing. There were three intermediate stations at Acton Green (now Chiswick Park), Mill Hill Park (now Acton Town) and Ealing Common & West Acton (now just Ealing Common). Services began on 1st July 1879, giving a running time between Mansion House and Ealing of 48 minutes.

As soon as work on the extension started, landowners in the areas of Isleworth and Hounslow saw an opportunity to cash in on the increase in land prices which always seemed to follow the coming of the railway. A new company, the Hounslow & Metropolitan Railway, was formed to build a line from Hounslow Barracks (whose site was at the car park of the present Hounslow West) to a junction with the Ealing extension at Mill Hill Park. The choice of terminus was partly to attract custom from travellers approaching Hounslow from the west along the Bath Road, as well as to serve the barracks, but the line missed the town itself.

Second thoughts about the scheme as it stood seemed to have led to the deposition of a Bill to authorise a line from the main branch at what became Lampton Junction via a station at Hounslow Town to connect with the LSWR Kingston loop line just west of Twickenham. There was to be a connecting curve to the LSWR Hounslow line where they crossed. The line was opened from Mill Hill Park as far as Hounslow Town on 1st May 1883, two months before then Hounslow Town section had been authorised by its Act.

The station was built on an embankment which ended in a bridge abutment on the north side of Hounslow High Street ready for its extension south. This never came, due to serious opposition from the South Western, who regarded the intrusion into their territory as unacceptable, especially since they were giving the District running powers between Hammersmith and Turnham Green to get there in the first place.

The original route to the Barracks seems to have taken second place as it was built as a single line and was not doubled throughout until 1925. Services to Hounslow Barracks began on 21st July 1884, at first operating as a shuttle from Osterley & Spring Grove. A siding for locomotives was provided between the tracks just east of the station, the site now occupied by the present Osterley station, which replaced the old station on 25th March 1934.

Hounslow Town was closed on 31st March 1886 and was replaced by a new station at Heston Hounslow which was opened on the Hounslow Barracks line the next day. The train service now operated between Hounslow Barracks and Mill Hill Park until Hounslow Town was re-opened on 1st March 1903.

Development along the Hounslow line was slow during the late nineteenth and early twentieth centuries. It was only after the first world war that new housing really started to grow with any pace. It was perhaps a little too far west with so much development taking place along the line between Earl's Court and Ealing. Here the

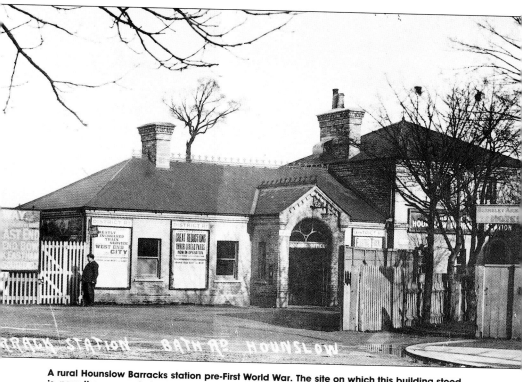

A rural Hounslow Barracks station pre-First World War. The site on which this building stood is now the car park for Hounslow West. The station was renamed in December 1925.
LT Museum

plan to get dwellers off the valuable commercial land in the city was working. They were willing to move out to the country to get better accommodation and their landlords were pleased to see them go. The railways provided transport for them to get to and from work and they also began to use them for shopping and leisure travel.

The leisure aspect of the District's operations first came to the fore with the opening of their 1¾ mile extension from West Brompton to Putney Bridge, then known as Fulham & Putney. It was authorised in 1878 and opened for traffic on 1st March 1880. It is interesting to note that the train service was half-hourly to the City for the first month but, from 1st April, two additional trains per hour were run to High Street Kensington. This service was the origin of the present day service between Wimbledon and Edgware Road.

The access to the River Thames at Putney was a source of leisure revenue for the District. People travelled there for steamboat trips on the river and for national events like the boat race. As with the Hammersmith and Ealing extensions, an increase in house building followed the opening of the line but it was noted in later years that the level of first class traffic was not as good as on the Ealing line because the areas served were not considered of such good class. In those days, most houses were built by developers and then rented, even to the better off families of Ealing. House ownership by the ordinary man was not to become common until the housing boom of the 1930s.

**A nine-coach train on the Wimbledon branch.** LT Museum U16184

The District wanted to get still further south and soon became embroiled in a scheme to build a Kingston & London Railway in a south-westerly direction from its terminus at Putney Bridge across Wimbledon Common, through Norbiton to Surbiton on the LSWR. The scheme was authorised in 1881 under a separate company title but became a joint venture between the District and LSWR the following year. However, as always, the District was in financial difficulties, unable to raise the money to pay for its half of the cost and no work was started.

Eventually, after three more years of intermittent discussion and following complaints from the residents of Wimbledon that a line across the common did nothing for them, the LSWR agreed to build a re-routed version of the line to Wimbledon and granted the District running powers over the line provided the District preserved the right of the LSWR to run to High Street and South Kensington. Work started on building the line in 1887 and it was opened to traffic on 3rd June 1889, with the trip from Wimbledon to Mansion House taking 48 minutes. The LSWR never took up its running powers over the District but it let the District run to Wimbledon.

The District's early strategy for getting to Windsor and Uxbridge had been through the double track connection with the Great Western at Ealing Broadway but this failed with the withdrawal of the Windsor service from 30th September 1885, partly due to poor receipts and partly to the difficulties of inter-working with GWR services over the flat junction. The poor patronage was possibly due to the rough riding of the District's four-wheel carriages on the non-stop run between Ealing and Slough. After the service ceased the connection was maintained, indirectly after the Central Line tracks were opened in 1917 but it was finally removed in 1972. The next target was to be Uxbridge with its own railway. Two companies were set up; the first was the Ealing and South Harrow Railway (incorporated in 1894), the second the Harrow and Uxbridge Railway (1897). Both companies were to be managed by the District.

**District steam trains passing on the Ealing line.** Lens of Sutton

The Ealing and South Harrow was to run from a junction with the District's Ealing line at Hanger Lane through the farm lands and open countryside to Roxeth (the area now known as South Harrow). The Harrow and Uxbridge line was to be a continuation from there. There was also to be a connection from Ealing Broadway to North Ealing but this was never built. Work on the Ealing and South Harrow began in 1898 and was completed at the end of 1899 but it was not opened throughout to the public until 28th June 1903. By then, the District had acquired a new management team and the line had been electrified as a test bed for the conversion of the whole railway.

In the meantime, the Harrow and Uxbridge company started negotiations with the Metropolitan following their realisation that the District was already overstretched financially and was preoccupied with the possibility of electrification and with building the Whitechapel & Bow Railway, of which more later. However, the company retained a clause in their new agreement which allowed the District to run trains over the line to Uxbridge if they wished. The line was eventually opened by the Metropolitan in 1905 with a connection between Rayners Lane and the Metropolitan at Harrow-on-the-Hill. It was linked to the E&SH at South Harrow but the link was not used until 1910.

The final western District project was the Acton Loop Line, later to become known as the South Acton branch. It was first proposed in 1878 but nothing was done, apart from land purchase, until, after a 20-year delay, construction began in 1898. Work on building the short connection between the District on the eastern side of Mill Hill Park to the North and South Western Junction Railway just north of South Acton station was completed in February 1899. It was opened for traffic in May but it was only used for the transfer of materials to the Ealing and South Harrow Line. It was opened for passenger traffic under electric traction on 13th June 1905. Although the line was double-tracked, District trains were confined to a single platform at South Acton.

# The District in the East

Although the eastern terminus of the District remained at Mansion House for over 20 years, the original 1864 Act sanctioning the formation of the Metropolitan District Railway authorised the building of the line as far as Tower Hill. The Metropolitan Railway was also authorised to build its share of the eastern end of the Circle between Moorgate and Tower Hill but neither company had the money to put into such expensive tunnelling schemes. Once the two companies had separated, the Metropolitan regarded the completion of the Circle as detrimental to its interests. It feared its traffic receipts over the profitable northern side of the Circle would be diluted once the District got access at the eastern end and it tried to get Parliament to authorise it to abandon the unbuilt section east of Moorgate.

Business interests in the City became so exasperated with the Metropolitan over its attitude that they formed a separate company, the Metropolitan Inner Circle Completion Railway, which was incorporated in 1874 to finish the job. The Metropolitan responded by hurriedly reviving their original scheme so as not to be left out of the action but they were too late. The MICCR had to persuade the local authorities in the City to contribute some money to help with associated street improvements. They also gained the support of the District, who offered to work the railway, and their proposal became authorised.

The Metropolitan, realising that it was in their interests to get their part of the Circle built, pushed east with an extension to Bishopsgate (opened 12th July 1875) and now called Liverpool Street) and on to Aldgate on 18th November 1876. At the same time, they still discouraged investment in the MICCR scheme, which remained without the necessary capital to begin work. Watkin of the Metropolitan sought to deal directly with the District in the hope of securing a better deal than he might get through the MICCR and a joint committee was set up by the District and Metropolitan boards. It eventually agreed on a scheme to complete the Inner Circle together with a connection to the East London Railway near Whitechapel. The City Lines and Extensions, as the scheme became known, was authorised by an Act of 1879.

There was considerable delay in starting the work. There were various agreements to be formed over the extent of the railway's involvement in the street improvements required as part of the scheme and in proposals to burrow under buildings rather than purchase and demolish them. The Metropolitan, although agreeing to the joint scheme, obtained separate parliamentary sanction in 1881 to build its own extension to Tower station, on the site of the present Tower Hill. Seeing the work on this section start spurred the District into action to get the money for its half of the remaining City Lines and Extensions work, and, by the time the Metropolitan opened its extension on 25th September 1882, work on the section between the Tower and Mansion House had started in earnest.

The original intention had been to build a line from a junction with the Circle at Minories to a south facing junction with the East London Railway at Whitechapel with intermediate stations at Aldgate East and St Marys. A connecting curve between the Circle just west of Aldgate station and the new line east of Aldgate East was also to

**The terminus at Whitechapel, c.1890.**

be built. An additional terminal station was built by the District at Whitechapel to replace its terminus at Mansion House which was to become a through station with two bay roads.

The first section to open was the line from the East London Railway, which opened on 1st January 1884 only as far as St Marys. On 6th October the same year, the connections through to the Circle were opened and the Circle itself was completed. New stations were opened at Cannon Street, Monument, Mark Lane, Aldgate East and Whitechapel. The original Metropolitan station at Tower was closed the following week, the new station (Mark Lane) just to the west being its replacement. Mark Lane was renamed Tower Hill on 1st September 1946 and was finally replaced by a new station on 5th February 1967 on the site of the original Metropolitan Tower station but now called Tower Hill.

From 6th October 1884 District trains worked through from the southern side of the Circle to Whitechapel or New Cross, East London Railway, a station closed on 31st August 1886, from which time trains ran into New Cross (LB&SCR, now New Cross Gate), whilst Metropolitan trains worked from the northern side to New Cross (South Eastern Railway). This service ceased on 31st July 1905. Both companies henceforth also worked right round the Circle.

The path to completion of the Circle had not been easy and neither was its day-to-day working. Apart from the difficulties of making all the various services slot in with each other through the various flat junctions at Aldgate, South Kensington and Earl's Court amongst others, there were constant disputes about the interpretation of the joint working agreements. To begin with, the Metropolitan tried to get the District to pay for the bulk of its costs incurred in opening and operating the extension from Aldgate to The Tower. The Met went to court but only got a part settlement. Ticketing, train operations, expenses and property rights all figured in various lengthy litigation processes which were conducted on behalf of both companies over the next few years. In different cases, both the District and Metropolitan were winners and losers. Perhaps the only real gainers were the lawyers.

For virtually the whole time from the District's breaking apart from the Metropolitan in 1871 until the start of electrification work in 1903, the two railways conducted their operations in a state of mutual hostility, often resorting to the courts to settle their differences. The degree of hostility waxed and waned over the years, but one high point was in May 1886, when any unsuspecting passenger booking an Inner Circle ticket was invariably sent by the route which entailed a journey, direct or otherwise, over the line owned by the company issuing the ticket (at joint stations each railway had its own booking office). This was accompanied by a belligerent poster campaign inducing the passenger to book by the route which best suited either the District or the Metropolitan.

Even with the opening of the complete Circle Line, revenue for the District was still not enough to enable shareholders to get a reasonable return. Working costs over the City extensions were high and there was, anyway, a general economic depression which was not even lifted by the celebration of Queen Victoria's Golden Jubilee in 1887. Bus competition was a factor in the trouble for the District, burdened as it was with the debts of its inner city construction, and more trouble was to come. The opening of the electrically operated City and South London tube railway in 1890, the year after the District's south western route to Wimbledon opened, was to demonstrate even more how inhospitable were the steam filled tunnels of the Circle.

In line with its policy of expansion to enable traffic to be drawn into central London to help pay for the tunnel costs, the District joined the London Tilbury & Southend Railway in 1897 to promote a Whitechapel & Bow Railway.

The LT&S line between Bow Common (later Gas Factory) Junction and Barking had been opened on 31st March 1858. LT&S trains to Southend and Tilbury used the Eastern Counties Railway (which became the Great Eastern Railway in 1862) terminus at Fenchurch Street. They had previously been routed via Stratford and Woodgrange Park but henceforth ran over the new line via Bromley, Plaistow and East Ham.

The Whitechapel & Bow was to be built in tunnel eastwards from the District terminus at Whitechapel under the Mile End and Bow Roads for two miles until it rose to the surface up a 1 in 45 gradient to connect with the LT&SR at Campbell Road. It would give the District access to the eastern countryside to balance their lines in the west.

Recognition that electrification was a distinct possibility was evident in the proposal for the new line which included powers to work the line electrically and provision of land at Bromley for a power station. Work on the line began in 1899 and it was opened to traffic on 2nd June 1902. There were three intermediate stations at Stepney Green (opened 23rd June), Mile End (opened 2nd June) and Bow Road (opened 11th June). Trains worked over the new line to the LT&SR through to East Ham. A few trains even ran as far as Upminster. The subsequent history of the line was to become bound up in the electrification of the District.

# Trains and Services in Steam Days

When the District began operating its own trains from 3rd July 1871, up to 12 trains an hour operated out of Mansion House. Half of these were worked round the 'Inner Circle' by the Metropolitan to its terminus at Moorgate, the other half to West Brompton. From 1st February 1872, the London & North Western Railway began working a half-hourly 'Outer Circle' service from Mansion House to Broad Street via Earl's Court, Addison Road and Willesden. They had contributed towards the construction costs of Mansion House and had exclusive rights to the south bay road there. A 'Middle Circle' was introduced by agreement with the Great Western Railway whose trains ran half hourly from Mansion House to Moorgate via Earl's Court, Addison Road and Paddington. These trains were worked by District locomotives between Mansion House and Earl's Court where GW engines took over. Both services lasted into the 20th century, although the Middle Circle was cut back to Earl's Court after 30th June 1900 and ceased altogether on 31st January 1905.

When the western branches were opened, each had a standard half-hourly service to Mansion House at first, with the exception of the Hounslow service. This only ever went to Earl's Court, apart from a short time after its opening in May 1883, and was usually only an hourly service with an extra train at peak times.

The Putney service was also opened with a half-hourly frequency, but after only a month an additional two trains an hour ran between Putney Bridge and High Street Kensington. By the time the extension to Wimbledon was opened on 3rd June 1889, the District had a new terminus at Whitechapel and the bulk of the services went there. Some trains from the west were terminated at High Street or South Kensington and some went through to New Cross (LB&SCR).

When the Inner Circle was completed in 1884, the standard service was six trains per hour in each direction. At first, the District worked alternate trains with the Metropolitan but later the Metropolitan took over all the outer rail workings while the District worked most of the inner rail — the anti-clockwise service — to try to balance the proportion of mileage to ownership.

It was normal for all trains to stop at all stations. Only rarely did special journeys or very early morning trains miss any stops. On Sundays, it was standard practice on the District, as it was on most other local railway services, to have a two-hour 'Church Interval' between 11.00 and 13.00. This was abandoned on 26th July 1903.

In the strange way history has of repeating itself, smoking carriages were not provided on the District during its early years. The no smoking rule was rigidly enforced on many railways and arguments both amongst passengers and between passengers and staff, even fights, sometimes followed complaints about smoking. Things got so bad that it was decided to introduce a law which forced railways to provide smoking accommodation. It was introduced with the Regulation of Railways Act 1868, but the Metropolitan succeeded in getting a dispensation for itself and the District until it eventually succumbed to the weight of public opinion. Smoking compartments were first provided on District trains in 1874 and lasted until the general ban on smoking on Underground trains in 1984.

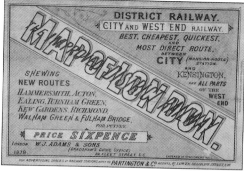

**Front and back covers of District Railway map of 1879.**
Alan Blake

A year before the agreement whereby the Metropolitan worked the District's train services was due to end in July 1871, the District began looking for suitable trains of its own. The most obvious choice was to go for the same type as used by the Metropolitan, which had been specially designed for operation in tunnels. The District therefore ordered, in November 1870, twenty-four locomotives very similar in design to those operated by the Metropolitan. They were so similar, being painted in the same olive green and with no external marks of ownership, that they were originally allocated identification letters instead of the usual numbers. They were built by Beyer Peacock & Co. of Manchester and were of the 4-4-0 tank type, with 5ft 9in driving wheels. In full working order, they weighed about 46 tons. The original locomotives had wrought iron boilers with a working pressure of 130 lbs psi. They had two 17in x 24in cylinders and cost £2280 each.

**Standard District Railway Steam locomotive. Some 54 of these were built by Beyer Peacock between 1871 and 1886. For tunnel working, steam condensing equipment was provided.**

The locomotive situation seems to have been somewhat overstretched during the early years as six more engines were ordered in November 1875 and were delivered during the summer of 1876. These had 160lb boilers and shorter fireboxes and were fitted with cabs for a time until the crews complained that they did not like them. Further batches of six at a time were delivered in 1881, 1883, 1884 and 1886 until the company had a total of 54 machines.

**District Railway four-wheeled steam stock at Lillie Bridge depot. The teak bodies were varnished.** LT Museum

The passenger stock represented a departure from the Metropolitan's adopted design. The Metropolitan used 8-wheeled carriages which had soon exhibited signs of difficulty with sharp curves, so the District, following the advice of its newly appointed director, J.S. Forbes, chose 4-wheeled vehicles. These, not surprisingly as Forbes was also London Chatham & Dover Railway General Manager, closely resembled some vehicles belonging to that railway. The District ordered 19 x 8-coach sets, each consisting of two first class, two seconds and four thirds, a total of 152 vehicles. All measured 26½ft long over the body and 29ft 2in over the buffers. The original vehicles were built on underframes made up of wood and wrought iron. Subsequent orders had all wrought iron underframes.

First class coaches had four compartments each seating five a side. Second and third class had five compartments also seating five a side. The only upholstery provided in the third class consisted of a strip of carpeting on the seat and a padded strip at the back of the seat at shoulder height. Second classes had slightly better upholstery but the first class was more roomy with sprung stuffed seating and full height padding. Half the coaches were built by the Oldbury Carriage Company, the other half by the Gloucester Wagon Company. The District, being short of cash, bought the carriages on hire purchase through a finance house calling itself the Railway Rolling Stock Company. It took them until 1878 to pay off the debt.

The 19 trains delivered in 1871 were more than enough to operate the services planned by the District in the foreseeable future. At first, only about 12 were needed and it was only when the Ealing extension was being built that more trains were ordered. Two were ordered from Ashbury's and two from the Metropolitan Railway Carriage & Wagon Co. and were delivered in 1879. By this time, the company had decided to operate 9-coach trains, so the new trains were built using the original formation expanded by an additional second class coach. Some 8-coach sets appear to have been converted to 9-coach formation from 1877 and some trains on the less well patronised services were run with 4- or 5-coach sets.

Interior of Third Class steam stock brake coach as restored for the District's diamond jubilee exhibition.
LT Museum

In November 1880, a further six 9-coach sets were ordered from Oldbury, apparently in anticipation of completion of the Circle. They were delivered in 1881, followed by a further six sets in each of the years 1883 and 1884 from Ashbury. Oldbury was out of favour by this time due to their excessive claims for variations during their 1881 order. Two more trains by the Metropolitan Railway Carriage & Wagon Co. were delivered in 1891.

For the opening of the Whitechapel & Bow Railway on 2nd June 1902, Ashbury built a further six trains, half of which were to be owned by the LT&SR and half by the District. Unlike the earlier stock, these trains had steel frames and were provided with proper guards vans in a third class brake coach. They were finished in a deep maroon colour, in contrast to the plain varnish of the original District stock.

District trains were originally provided with mechanically operated brakes applied from the engine or by the guards from special compartments in the end coaches of the train. Between 1874 and 1876, an air operated braking system by Westinghouse was fitted. It was the first installation of its kind in the country, but it was not automatic in the event of a train break-away or other emergency. In spite of the company's forward thinking regarding brakes, they received a letter from the Board of Trade in 1880 asking them to fit an automatic or continuous brake but it was not until 1890-92 that the improved (fail-safe) version of the same manufacturer's brake was installed. It subsequently became the standard safety braking system for the Underground until its replacement in the 1970s by a new standard electrically controlled emergency braking system.

Train lighting was originally by coal gas burners supplied from bags mounted in wooden frames on the roofs of the coaches. The gas was replenished at the end of each trip from the mains at Mansion House and High Street Kensington stations. When the line was extended to Hammersmith, a special gas main was laid from the gas making plant at Lillie Bridge to the new station. In 1880, a system using compressed oil gas was experimentally introduced on a train. It was called the Pintsch Patent Gas system and its efficiency convinced the board to replace the old gas bags. Each coach was provided with a cylindrical gas cylinder which was charged at night from gas holders which were taken on trucks to various points around the system where trains were recharged for the next day's service. The conversion to the new system was carried out during 1881-82.

Towards the end of steam haulage, some trials were carried out with electric lighting systems. In 1890, negotiations were conducted with 'The Railway Automatic Electric Syndicate' over the provision of electric reading lamps but the experiment was not a success and ended in a legal battle fought by the District to get £1300 of its money back. Later, a trial set of Stone's dynamos, driven off the coach axles and backed up by batteries, were fitted to a train but the anticipated electrification forestalled any general conversion scheme for the rest of the stock.

In 1894, to overcome passenger complaints about the difficulty of seeing station names in the smoke and gloom of the tunnel amongst the plethora of advertising hoardings mounted on every available flat surface, a trial was carried out of a train mounted station indicator. Frames to carry the indicators were installed in the partitions between compartments on each coach. The station names were changed by the guard operating a cable and advertisements appeared between the station names. Realising that the guards would sometimes forget to change the signs, the system suppliers, The Railway Station Indicator Company, introduced a version operated by treadles on the track. The system was installed on a number of trains between 1897 and 1899 but it proved very difficult to maintain in good working order and was abandoned following an adverse report to the board in September 1899.

**Sloane Square station at the turn of the century.** Lens of Sutton

# Moves to Electric Power

By the mid 1890s, it was quite obvious that the District could no longer afford to ignore the public's pressure for substantial improvements to their travelling conditions. The atmospheric pollution in the tunnels was the most common cause of complaint and can only be imagined today, but there were other issues, like the lack of train heating and, particularly, overcrowding at certain times of day. The inability of the existing line to carry more trains was recognised as early as 1879 when the District obtained authority to double the tunnel section of the line, but there was no money available for what would be a very expensive project.

Although some attempts had been made to improve matters for passengers by such devices as station indicators and heaters fitted to trains, these were only scratching at the surface of the problem. What the public really wanted was the grand clean up, modernisation, in other words, electrification. They were demonstrating their dissatisfaction and voting with their feet. Traffic levels began to suffer during the late 1890s as passengers were lost to the buses, particularly during the summer. These factors, combined with the need to increase line capacity, led to a revival of the track doubling proposal. In 1897 powers were sought to build a double track tube line under the existing main line between Earl's Court and Mansion House. The line was to be operated by cable or electric traction. A cheaper alternative being considered at the same time was the electrification of the existing line. All that was needed was the money for the job.

The Metropolitan Railway was under the same sort of pressure as the District, but they had, since 1887, actually looked at various electrification schemes offered to them by hopeful contractors and had even tried an experiment at Wembley Park. What was needed was for the Circle, the District and Metropolitan to agree on a compatible electric traction system, a difficult prospect in view of their long history of conflict. However, in May 1898, a joint agreement was finalised to carry out a trial of electric traction. Work began at once. The line between Earl's Court and High Street Kensington was selected as the test site. A small power station was built at track level at the Warwick Road end of Earl's Court station and a 6-coach train was ordered from Brown Marshall & Co. with electrical equipment from Siemens. The tracks were fitted with two conductor rails, one positive and one return, both located outside the running rails and supplied with direct current from the power station.

The train was delivered early in 1900. It consisted of two motor coaches, weighing 54 tons apiece, and four trailers weighing 18 tons each. Half the train was owned by the District and half by the Metropolitan. The District's half represented the first bogie vehicles owned by the company but they were never given numbers and never recorded in the company's books.

During February 1900 various trials were carried out to compare one of the motor coaches with a steam locomotive. It was noted at the time as being 'superior in every way'. The train, formed with a motor coach at each end of the set of four trailers, entered public service on 21st May 1900, passengers being charged one shilling (5p) for the privilege. It was imagined that people would consider it a novelty and would be prepared to pay extra. However much it may have been a novelty to the Metropolitan

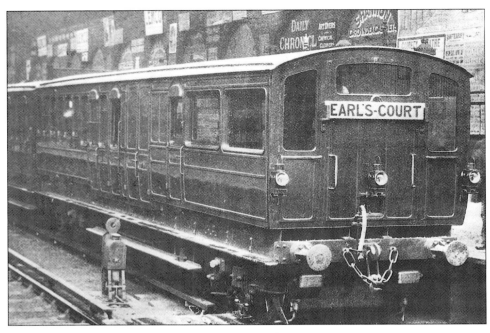

**The experimental electric train at Earl's Court in 1900.** LT Museum

and District management, Londoners knew differently. They had already seen electric traction on the City & South London Railway over the previous ten years and on the Waterloo & City Line since 1898. As a trip on the District's experimental train cost three times the ordinary first class fare, it ran practically empty for the first week. After that, the fares were brought down to normal levels. The train ran until 6th November 1900.

The train consisted of two power coaches with four trailer coaches between them. Each power vehicle was a self-contained electric locomotive with the control equipment in a compartment behind the driver's cab and the motors mounted directly on the axles. There was no remote control of the rear coach from the front, so it was towed by the front coach as if it were a trailer. The lack of through control, later to become known as multiple unit control, was much criticised by engineers at the time.

Although the experiment with Siemen's equipment was deemed a success, it was decided that the job of electrifying the Circle should go out to tender. For the time being, electrification of the rest of the District or Metropolitan was not included. Nine companies put in bids, the 3000 volt three-phase alternating current system by the Hungarian firm Ganz & Company being accepted by the Metropolitan and District boards in December 1900. However, the problem of finance had yet to be resolved.

The Metropolitan had the money to start work, but the District was almost bankrupt. To raise money, one of the District's largest shareholders, Mr R.W. Perks, had, on his own initiative but doubtless with the blessing of the District's Chairman Forbes, taken an opportunity to interest certain American financiers in the possibilities of electrification and the money that might be made from it.

As a result of Perks' efforts, the banking house of Speyer Brothers, with Charles Tyson Yerkes and other interested US financiers, formed a syndicate with him and started laying the foundations of a takeover. They began by providing the funding of the Ealing & South Harrow Railway and the District's share of the Whitechapel & Bow line. It was probably their interest in electrification which prevented the District purchasing new steam locomotives for these lines. They had gone as far as ordering seven engines from Dubs & Co in September 1900 for the W & B but they cancelled them in 1901. Although they purchased coaches for the W & B, jointly with the LT & SR, they never bought any rolling stock for the E & SH, and the line remained unused for almost four years after its completion.

Early in 1901, the Speyer-Yerkes-Perks Group set up the Metropolitan District Electric Traction Company with Yerkes as largest shareholder and Chairman. The sole purpose of the company was to electrify the District. They soon got an agreement with the District over terms for electrification and had it sanctioned by Parliament under the District Railway Act of August 1901. The Electric Traction Company would electrify the whole of the District in return for a payment of 4% per annum on the capital cost until it was paid off. The District had effectively been taken over. The new group, knowing there was going to be trouble, made sure the agreement included a proviso that any disputes with the Metropolitan over the traction system to be used would go to independent arbitration.

By this time Forbes knew that his Americans would not want the Ganz system. Although it appeared cheap, it was relatively new and involved alternating current and twin overhead wires in the tunnels of the Circle. On the other hand, both Britain and the US had already had several years of direct current traction on railways and tramways and it was this which was envisaged in the new agreement. It even spoke about current rails as opposed to wires. Yerkes had already been involved in several DC electrification schemes in the US and had brought in James Russell Chapman, an American electrification expert, as his chief engineer. He would not have agreed to lead the financing of the District's electrification had he not got their agreement to use DC traction.

**Arrangement of conductor rails.**

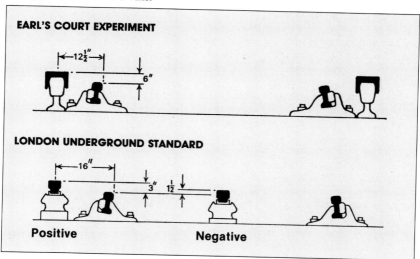

At first sight, the Metropolitan appears to have been left out of all this but John J. Mellor, then Chairman of the Metropolitan, was well aware of the situation as he was in constant touch with Forbes during the electrification trials. It was also known that not everyone was enamoured of the Ganz system. The Board of Trade inspectors had already expressed reservations about it and, even after visits to Switzerland to see a version of the AC system working, not everyone was sure that it was right for the Inner Circle. It is recorded that, as a result of tests of Ganz equipment witnessed by Yerkes at Lecco, he refused to have anything further to do with the system. In spite of this, the Metropolitan stuck to its guns and insisted on proceeding with the AC system as originally agreed.

The issue went to arbitration almost before the Electric Traction Company's agreement with the District had become enacted. A special tribunal was set up on 18th September 1901 and the final judgement was officially communicated to the Boards of the two railways on 12th December 1901. It was no surprise to anyone (except perhaps to some of the Metropolitan's directors) that the tribunal found in favour of the District's 630 volt DC system using third and fourth conductor rails. Work on equipping the line began almost at once, starting with the Ealing & South Harrow Railway. This was to become the testing ground for the equipment and for a new signalling system which was to be part of the scheme.

The District's future was based on improving the two most critical areas of its operation — conversion to electric traction to eliminate the smoke and dirt from the tunnels and resignalling to improve the capacity and eliminate overcrowding. Before the main line was electrified both systems were tried out on the Ealing & South Harrow line and then opened to the public. The first section opened between Mill Hill Park and Park Royal in time for the Royal Agricultural Society's Show on 23rd June 1903 and, five days later, public service was extended through to South Harrow.

By this time the Traction Company had been absorbed by a new company called the Underground Electric Railways of London Ltd (UERL), which also acquired the three tube lines then under construction or planned, the Bakerloo, Piccadilly and Hampstead tubes. This new combination of tube railway companies with the District led to the District giving the Piccadilly tube line the rights to use the authorised deep level tube route between Earl's Court and South Kensington but it retained the right to use it if it wanted to build the line through to Mansion House. As can still be seen at the eastern end of the station, the tunnels at South Kensington were arranged to allow the future building of junctions with the Mansion House line. The new combine, which became known as the 'Underground Group', adopted a common electrification system, used power provided by a common power house at Lots Road, Chelsea and had a common signalling system.

The combine was based at the offices over the District station at St James's Park. The District headquarters had moved into offices specially built over the station in 1898, the construction of which had included a new entrance in Palmer Street. These offices were completely rebuilt in 1929 to a design by Charles Holden. Ten sculptures were mounted on the exterior of the building, the artists commissioned to do them including Eric Gill, Eric Aumonier, Jacob Epstein and Henry Moore. At platform level the station was retiled in the style of the period. More recently, a scheme to improve security to the entrance of the London Transport head offices and to let some of the ground floor space for retail shops has led to a less convenient entrance from Broadway to the station.

# Resignalling

The District's original signalling system was based on that invented by C.E. Spagnoletti, signalling superintendent on the Great Western Railway, and adopted by the Metropolitan Railway. The line was divided into 'block sections', each controlled by a signalman. Each train was passed from one section to the next by the signalmen communicating through the 'block telegraph'. Signals and points were mechanically locked to prevent conflicting moves but there was no locking to prevent a second train being accepted into an occupied section. To overcome this, from the early 1880s the block telegraph instruments were converted by the firm of Sykes to be electrically interlocked with signals.

The new signalling installed with electrification was the latest technology imported from America and based on that first introduced on the Boston Elevated Railroad in 1900. It used track circuits to operate signals automatically with the passage of the trains. Its first recorded use on the District seems to have been a trial on the Hounslow branch in 1901. Instead of being cleared by a signalman for the passage of each train as normally, the new system allowed a signal to remain cleared until the detection of a train on the track circuit caused it to go to danger. It automatically cleared again when the train had left the section it was protecting. With this system, signalmen were only required at junctions.

A full scale installation was tried on the South Harrow branch in 1903 and the rest of the District was converted by January 1906. The system included mechanical trainstops which caused an irretrievable brake application as a train passed a danger signal. The Metropolitan began using a version of it from 1908 and it was eventually adopted on all the tube lines.

**Earl's Court East signal box spanning the tracks east of Earl's Court station. This box was replaced in 1957.**

The new signalling pioneered by the District was a success from the start. Automation had provided the extra capacity required by allowing 30 trains per hour instead of the 20 obtained under manual block working in steam days and there was a significant reduction in the number of signal boxes. Apart from some technical improvements, the basic principles have remained virtually unchanged to the present day, even being adapted in the 1960s for automatic train operation on the Victoria Line. Only in recent times has it been necessary to look for a more sophisticated system which has less reliance on mechanical parts and meets more stringent safety requirements while maintaining or even improving line capacity.

A big advantage of the system was that the track circuit status could be repeated in the signal box. A diagram over the lever frame displayed to the signalman whether the tracks in his area were free or occupied so he could operate all day without having to see his trains. The first such diagram in Britain was installed as part of the resignalling at Mill Hill Park in 1905.

With the new signalling, the identity of each train was fed by the signalman at the terminus to equipment which passed it along the line in advance of the train concerned. The District exploited this scheme to help passengers by displaying the train's destination on a platform mounted display — the 'Next Train Indicator'. At the busier stations the next three trains were indicated. Eventually, other Underground lines adopted a similar system, which is still in use today, but using electronic equipment instead of an electromechanical system.

In spite of its new train description apparatus, the District retained its steam-age system of front end lamps to display the train's destination. Sometimes referred to as Headcodes by other railways but as marker lights (an American term) by the District, these displays were based on the train's destination. The frequency of services was such that further identification was provided from 1908 with the introduction of train 'set numbers' and plates, showing also whether the train was non-stop or 'all stations'.

**Mill Hill Park station in the days of steam on the District. The station was widened to 3 tracks for electrification in 1905 and was renamed Acton Town in 1910. It was rebuilt by the Underground Group in 1932 when the Piccadilly Line was extended westwards from Hammersmith.** Lens of Sutton

# Exhibitions

For many years, an important source of income for the District was from exhibitions. These became popular from the 1870s, when improved travel in London made them accessible to a larger section of the public. The District served the South Kensington Exhibition grounds behind the Royal Albert Hall (hence Exhibition Road) and, on 4th May 1885, opened the subway between there and South Kensington station. Passengers were charged a penny toll, although the charge was included in through travel and admission tickets. Unfortunately the exhibitions ceased for ever in November 1886, as the land was needed to build the Imperial Institute. Henceforth the subway was opened on special occasions only, but was thrown open for free public use on 21st December 1908. In 1913 extra exits were opened to the Natural History Museum and the Victoria & Albert Museum.

A new site was leased by The American Exhibition Ltd (from 1888 it became The National Exhibitions Association Ltd) from the District Railway at Earl's Court. This included the triangle of land bounded by the West London Extension Railway and the District tracks to West Kensington and West Brompton, and a piece of land at the rear of Lillie Bridge Yard. The two sites were connected by a footbridge. The Empress Theatre was built on the latter site in 1895, named after the Empire of India Exhibition of that year. The site is now occupied by the Empress State Building.

A giant wheel was built on the Earl's Court site in 1895, similar to one erected for the World Fair in Chicago in 1893. It remained in use for 12 seasons until it was demolished by George Cohen in 1906. Following this, the larger exhibitions were transferred to a new site near Shepherd's Bush, the White City, where the Franco-British Exhibition opened in 1908. Smaller exhibitions at Earl's Court continued until 1913 when the District recovered its lease. During the First World War, the site was used by the Government as a clearing house for refugees. It was not returned fully to exhibition use until the present building was opened in September 1937.

Another exhibition venue was opened next to Addison Road station in 1886 with the completion of the Olympia building. Served by GWR Middle Circle and LNWR Outer Circle trains until electrification, this site provided a small but useful supplement to District earnings over the years. From 1905, the LNWR worked trains from Earl's Court and from 1914 these were electric, shuttling between Earl's Court and Willesden. This service ceased in 1940, following bomb damage just north of Addison Road. In December 1946, the District started a shuttle service to Olympia during the Bertram Mills Circus season. Until April 1986 the service ran only during such events but was then extended to a regular operation.

At various periods during the 19th century, the District arranged for bus services to connect its line to exhibitions and other important traffic centres. Services to Olympia from West Kensington ran for the Irish Exhibition in 1888-9 and in the following year for Barnum and Bailey's show. In 1890 buses ran between Sloane Square and Chelsea for the Military Exhibition and for the Naval Exhibition the following year. Other services were operated between Mansion House and Liverpool Street from June 1887, and two routes from Charing Cross (District) to Baker Street and Victoria to Baker Street (started November 1889).

# Electrification

As we have already seen, the Ealing & South Harrow line became the test bed for the District's electrification scheme. Two prototype multiple unit electric trains were built by the Brush Electrical Engineering Company of Loughborough.

The District's new electric trains were pure American in design. They had straight matchboarded sides, gated end entrance platforms, a pair of centrally positioned sliding doors, cast steel bogies, central buffing gear and clerestory roofs which curved down at the ends. Although later versions of this design were Anglicised to some extent, this basic design was to survive on the District for almost 70 years.

The two prototype trains, which were later classified A Stock in accordance with the District's custom of alphabetical identification of rolling stock, were a combination of two US designs. The car bodies were very similar to those built for the Boston Elevated Railway in 1901. The bogies were pure Chicago, being almost identical to the Hedley design used on the North Western Elevated Line in that city.

The two trains, some cars of which it was reported were painted in a bright yellow, were each formed of seven cars; three motor cars and four trailers. The motor cars had a pair of motors mounted on the leading car and a set of control equipment hung under the car. Only the driver's controls, switches and some fuses were mounted above floor level. One train had equipment supplied by British Thompson-Houston, the other by British Westinghouse, who later became Metropolitan Vickers. The control systems on both trains were based on the patents of Frank J. Sprague, who first tried his multiple unit control on the South Side Elevated Railway in Chicago in 1897. The BTH system, which used electro-magnetic contactors instead of the electro-pneumatic contactors of the BW system, became the standard for the District and was provided on all its clerestory-roofed stock.

For its main line electrification of 1905, the District was provided with 60 x 7-car trains of B Stock. Large numbers of the cars were built in France and Belgium, much to the disgust of British manufacturers who complained loudly. They were actually almost fully occupied building cars for the Metropolitan and other railways and tramways so there was only a little capacity available to fill part of the District's order. The District's new American management also complained that British firms were too vulnerable to industrial action — this complaint being made in 1904!

As with the A Stock, the American stamp on the new cars' design was unmistakable. They had Boston style bodies, even to the extent that they had copies of the enclosure of the end platforms, a modification then being undertaken on existing cars in Boston, and bogies were again Chicagoan, both motor and trailer types being to Frank Hedley's design. Couplers were also of Chicago origin. The A Stock had the Van Dorn design, which was little more than a link and pin, while the B Stock had Stearn and Ward's automatic mechanical type. The difference made it impossible for the two types to be coupled together until the A Stock was modified some years later.

Messrs Stearn and Ward had a patent on their coupler which netted them £1 for every one fitted. The UERL purchased over 2000 of them between 1904 and 1907 for the District and tube lines, making a comfortable sum for each man, probably equivalent at that time to a couple of year's salary. Hedley, the bogie designer, and Ward were part of the team of engineers brought over from America by Yerkes.

Hedley's cast steel bogies were not a success on the District and they were eventually superseded by traditional British designs, but Ward's coupler was the standard on the Underground for many years.

The B Stock had air operated doors. This was standard equipment for new cars in Chicago by this time but it met with little success in London. The District's installation lasted only three years. The movement of the doors was erratic and sharp and caused a number of injuries to passengers and their clothing. It is recorded that ladies wearing the long bustled dresses, fashionable at the time, were particularly vulnerable and there were some embarrassing incidents which apparently offended Edwardian decency. It also involved £8,000 a year extra in maintenance costs, which was then equivalent to the price of four new cars. The equipment was removed in 1908 and the doors were provided with self-balancing gear to allow simple hand operation by the passengers.

The door alterations had a curious effect on the use of crews. The air doors required the services of a 'gateman' who stood over the couplings between cars and operated the valves located on the car ends. Each man worked half the doors on two adjacent cars. When the equipment was removed, the crew was reduced from seven to three; rear guard, front guard and driver. Passengers were left to work the doors themselves.

Another idea imported onto the District which was quickly abandoned was the rule of reserving doors for entrance or exit. End doors were for entrance, centre doors for exit. Once the gatemen had been withdrawn, it became unenforceable and was soon allowed to lapse, although the notices over the doorways survived on some cars until the 1920s.

**Putney Bridge station before the first world war with a 1905 stock train in the platform.**

The B Stock cars were all built of wood but the motor cars were strengthened with steel underframes because of the additional loads placed on the structure by the traction equipment. However, by the time these cars were delivered in 1905, a number of constructors in both the US and Britain had successfully built some prototype steel-bodied cars. The improved strength and durability of steel over wooden cars was quickly recognised and later batches of cars for the District were steel-bodied.

To supply the power for the District's electrification, the Traction Company built a power station on the bank of the River Thames at Lots Road, Chelsea. It was also used to supply power to the Bakerloo, Piccadilly and Hampstead tube lines and has remained one of the principal sources of electric power for the Underground ever since.

With the introduction of electric traction the opportunity was taken to give passengers the clean environment they had so long pushed for. Stations had the soot removed and were repainted and had electric lighting installed.

Electrification transformed the District in terms of its equipment and the environment, particularly in the tunnels, but improvements in traffic levels were slow at first. Services began to be converted to electric traction from June 1905 when electric trains began working between South Acton and Hounslow. They then gradually spread throughout the system as the new rolling stock was delivered. By 5th November 1905, all the steam trains had been replaced except the LNWR trains to Mansion House which were hauled by electric locomotives from 4th December 1905.

With electrification, the District service to New Cross was withdrawn (on 31st July 1905) and electric trains ran to Whitechapel and East Ham. The LT&S line was quadrupled between Bromley and East Ham to accommodate the additional trains. On 1st April 1908, quadrupling and electrification was extended through to Barking. A depot for electric stock was built at East Ham and lasted until the site was cleared in 1958 for the building of the LT&S East Ham depot in preparation for the 25kv AC overhead electrification of the line.

There were some teething troubles. On 1st July 1905, when the Metropolitan began working electric trains round the District side of the Circle Line, their trains damaged the District's conductor rails and had to be replaced by steam for several weeks while modifications were made to their shoegear; it was 22nd September when the last steam hauled Circle train ran. Not that the District was immune from troubles. There were a number of cases of axle breakages during the early years and the cast steel bogies frames were also prone to fracture. The troubles with doors have already been mentioned. The introduction of new technology is never easy and it took time for the staff to get used to the new equipment.

During this period, traffic was depressed to some extent by competition from buses and trams and from the Central London Railway and receipts were also reduced by the abolition of second class accommodation and the resulting conversion of most of this traffic to third class. The District also lost some traffic to the Piccadilly tube railway, then called the Great Northern, Piccadilly & Brompton Railway, which was opened in 1906.

The Piccadilly line was built in tunnel between Finsbury Park and a point just west of West Kensington where it rose to the surface and a new joint District and Piccadilly station called Barons Court was built. The line paralleled the District between Barons Court and South Kensington. The District gave up some space at Hammersmith where the station was rebuilt to accommodate a terminus for the Piccadilly line on its northern side. The District was widened between there and Barons Court and the two northern tracks were used by the Piccadilly. The present two eastbound tracks at Barons Court station were then the eastbound and westbound Piccadilly tracks.

Apart from the space at Hammersmith, the District also gave up a large part of its depot at Lillie Bridge. With electrification a new depot was completed in 1905 for District electric trains at Ealing Common, although it was called Mill Hill Park Depot at first. The Piccadilly trains gained access to the depot at Lillie Bridge via the connection at the east end of West Kensington station. The District retained part of the site for engineer's trains and, as the Piccadilly area was really too small to accommodate the whole of the tube fleet, some maintenance work was carried out by the District at Ealing Common.

The District's financial position began to improve after things had settled down and the train services were speeded up in December 1907 to match the full capabilities of the electric stock. Some peak hour trains were classified as 'Non Stop' for the first time, although they were really semi-fast, passing groups of up to seven stations on a trip. Non Stopping became a regular feature of District services from this time until 1964.

Some astute business management was used during these years to help the meagre finances of the company. Some interesting assets were sold off without loss of operating capability, including the power cables between Earl's Court and the LT&S line, which were sold to the LT&SR, and a percentage of the electric rolling stock deemed necessary to work the LT&S portion of services east of Whitechapel. Although the cars were henceforth owned by the LT&S, they were maintained and operated by the District.

The bulk of the District's steam stock was disposed of after electrification. Some 368 carriages were offered for sale in 1905 and 291 of them were sold to dealers. Most of the rest were scrapped; a few were retained as works vehicles. The 54 steam locomotives were stored until 1906 apart from six which were used for works trains. Two (Nos. 33 and 34) survived until after the first world war, one lasting until 1925, the other until 1932.

The combination of electrification and new signalling considerably reduced trip times. In steam days, the journey from Ealing to Mansion House took 48 minutes but modernisation reduced this to 35 minutes. The trip from Richmond was reduced from 54 to 41 minutes. Throughout the network, travel times fell by roundly 25%. This, together with increases of two or three times in the number of trains serving the branches, led to the long awaited recovery in the District's fortunes. This recovery was driven by expansion of housing development.

# KEW
## GARDENS

# BY DISTRICT R<sup>LY</sup>
## DIRECT

# Expansion

Although there had been a general rise in property development on the western side of London, particularly in the Ealing and Chiswick areas, Hounslow had been rather slower to develop until the arrival of electric traction. It was further away from London than Ealing or Chiswick and the steam service had been rather infrequent and slow. After electrification, housing in the area began to boom and the population increased by 50% between 1901 and 1911. The District even began working trains through to Uxbridge over the Metropolitan Line from 1st March 1910. There was also a housing boom in the Ealing area during this period when the population almost doubled.

Traffic was also helped in off-peak periods by excursion traffic to the 'country' areas west and north west of London and by the through service to the seaside resort of Southend. For the 1905 electrification the District bought ten electric locomotives, to haul London and North Western coaches between Earl's Court and Mansion House. When this service was cut back to Earl's Court in 1909, the locomotives were temporarily switched to 'top and tail' Inner Circle trains, but from 1st June 1910 they found a more suitable role in hauling through Ealing–Southend trains as far as Barking, where a Tilbury steam locomotive took over. The trains were extended to Shoeburyness in about 1911. In 1912 the Tilbury company supplied two eight-coach centre-corridor trains for this service, notable for having two coaches with retention-type toilets. Ordinary Tilbury compartment stock was still used occasionally. The timings varied considerably over the years, but typically there were three return trains a day.

THE NEW CORRIDOR STOCK
WORKING ON THE

# THROUGH TRAINS
# EALING AND SOUTHEND

SERVICE INCREASED
FROM 1ST JUNE

Facing Page
**District Railway poster of 1923.**
LT Museum Y1329

Left **A 1910 poster advertising the through trains to Southend-on-Sea, which ran on the District until 1939. The picture shows the rear end of the train, which is being hauled by two small electric locomotives until it reaches Barking where steam takes over.** LT Museum Y387

**Park Royal station on the South Harrow branch, with a single-car train approaching from Alperton.** LT Museum H/16299

The day trip was popular as a form of relaxation in those days when car ownership was very rare and television and radio non-existent. Many resort cafes were opened during the summer in areas like Ealing, Ruislip and Osterley where families and school parties would visit to take the country air away from the smoke and pollution of the inner areas of the city where they lived and worked. So many birds and beasts were killed by District trains on the countrified South Harrow branch that the District set up a natural history collection of stuffed creatures in glass cases, which was displayed at Charing Cross in the 1920s. These included an otter caught in April 1911, a barn owl caught in November 1912, a nightjar, and two tawny owls, killed in March 1925.

**A two-car train of wooden-bodied stock at Northfields on the branch line to Hounslow before the first world war. This station was rebuilt in 1932 on the other side of the road bridge over the railway.**

A double-ended motor car of B Stock at Sudbury Town circa 1911. The District began a service to Uxbridge in 1910. When the B Stock was built for the District electrification in 1905 each 7-car train had a 'middle motor car' equipped with a driver's cab at each end.
Lens of Sutton

An early view inside Ealing Common depot, with pipework in progress and A stock lifted in the background. R.J. Greenaway collection

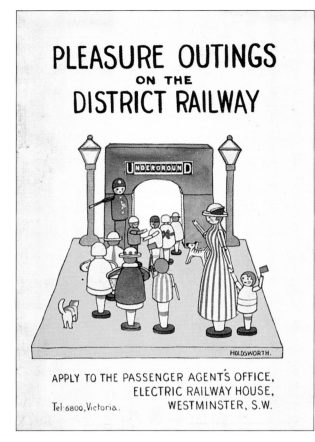

PLEASURE OUTINGS
ON THE
DISTRICT RAILWAY

UNDERGROUND

HOLDSWORTH.

APPLY TO THE PASSENGER AGENT'S OFFICE,
ELECTRIC RAILWAY HOUSE,
Tel: 6800, Victoria.       WESTMINSTER, S.W.

The cover of a small booklet giving details of special rates for parties using the District Railway for days out. Richmond, Kew Gardens, Horsenden Hill and the Paddocks pleasure park at South Harrow were among the places mentioned.

The increases in traffic soon led to congestion difficulties over the line between Hammersmith and Turnham Green which was still owned by the LSWR and was used by its trains and those of the GWR and Midland Railway. The LSWR agreed to double the line and gave the southern two tracks (now the westbound District and Piccadilly tracks) for the exclusive use of the District. A new grade-separated junction was opened at Turnham Green to allow Ealing trains to pass over the LSWR tracks to Richmond. The new lines were opened on 3rd December 1911 and an improved timetable with more trains and more non-stopping was introduced in the following week. The variety of stations non-stopped became so great that each car was fitted with an indicator board next to one of the end doorways which listed the stations under the heading 'Not Stopping at'.

The GWR steam service over this section was withdrawn in January 1911 and the LSWR Waterloo–Addison Road–Richmond service in 1916. After this the LSWR tracks were little used apart from the passage of goods or engineers' trains until, as we shall see, they found a new lease of life in 1932.

The increase in services in 1911 was supported by a new injection of rolling stock. A total of 112 new cars were ordered in three batches between 1910 and 1912 and were classified as the C, D and E Stocks. They were intended to work with the B

**A six-car train of pre-1914 Stock arriving at Northfields and Little Ealing to collect a party of children on a Sunday outing circa 1912.**

Stock and were broadly similar to them except that they had steel bodies and plate-frame or pressed steel bogies. The E Stock did not have the clerestory roof of the other stocks, a development intended to overcome complaints from passengers of draughts and incoming rainwater. Some cars were fitted with equipment from three of the electric locomotives which, although then only five years old, were withdrawn as surplus to requirements.

Soon after electrification, it was discovered that the 7-car formation did not allow for simple reductions in train lengths for off-peak traffic, a practice referred to as uncoupling, so in 1906 it was decided to provide some trailer cars with driving controls. These cars became known as Control Trailers or Driving Trailers and, during the 1920s, the District had a total of 32 of them. It was also decided to form trains of four, six or eight cars, each being provided with an equal number of motors and trailers, an arrangement which was to last until the early 1970s. The increase to 8-cars for certain peak hour trains meant that these trains were longer than most of the tunnel station platforms. To get all the passenger doors into the platforms at these stations, the driver had to position the train with his cab and the rear cab stopped in the tunnel. It was not until the 1960s that many of the platforms were extended to fully accommodate 8-car trains.

# The Great War

The District entered the era of the first world war in 1914 in better shape than it had ever been in its 46-year life. The technical problems of electrification and new signalling had settled down and the company had got used to the day-to-day running of a high volume, high frequency, rapid transit railway in the American style, albeit adapted to British methods. But, by the end of the war four years later, the railway was again in trouble. The war had generated very heavy traffic but, with men away at the war, the staff and materials necessary to keep the system in reasonable condition were not available. Maintenance was reduced to the level of casualty repairs and the rolling stock suffered considerably as a result. It also forcefully demonstrated the shortcomings of the wooden construction of the A and B Stocks.

Much of the stock was literally in a state of collapse. The wooden bodies were rotting away and could be seen sagging at the middle and ends. The trailers, which were almost entirely of wood, were particularly bad. Close inspection of the framework behind the panelling revealed that many of the main structural spars had been made up from several sections of timber spliced together. Over the years, the joints had loosened and left the body structurally unsound. Quality control during manufacture had obviously been very lax. Immediately after the war, work began on repairing those cars which were thought worth saving but some never survived and over 35 cars were withdrawn during the war and up to 1922.

In 1919, some Government assisted finance became available and the District took advantage of it to obtain 100 new cars of F Stock. It was unusual for its time in having three sets of double doors per car side and a very functional design. Compared with the earlier stocks, it looked very modern. It had a new arched roof body profile, a wide uncluttered interior with mostly longitudinal seating and oval windows in the car ends. Unfortunately, the passengers did not like it and the District, ever conscious of its fare-paying public, took the whole fleet of 100 cars through a refurbishment programme after only a year or so in service. The plain steel interiors and leather upholstery gave the cars a cold appearance so a professional designer was employed to produce a new colour scheme. The result was new patterned upholstery (lozenge pattern in third class) and the green and off-white finish which was applied to all Underground cars from this time and which lasted into the 1980s on the older trains. An example was applied to a Northern Line train in 1990 for that line's centenary celebrations.

Like any new stock entering service for the first time, the F Stock suffered its share of teething troubles. Apart from the complaints from passengers about the cold interior finish, the stock had a tendency to roll alarmingly and there were several incidents of trains striking station platforms. Modifications to stiffen the suspension soon cured this but a more serious problem with their power led to a rearrangement of the train formation. As delivered each 8-car train had three motor cars, each with two complete sets of traction equipment. The performance of these trains led to them catching up older trains and causing uneven gaps in the service. They were watered down by having a set of equipment removed from one of the motor cars. The story is told that the engineer responsible for the design of these cars was so ashamed of all the problems they developed that he committed suicide.

The F stock of 1921 was equipped with three sets of double doors per car side and was renowned as a crowd shifter. A three-car train is seen at South Ealing.
Lens of Sutton

This stock was intended to set new standards for the line, with better passenger capacity, more power than earlier stock and more doors to speed up station work. Unfortunately, the rest of the system never caught up with it. The signalling and power supplies both required improvements to allow the stock to be used to its full potential and these were not done. Nor were the older stocks upgraded to match. The F Stock was not compatible with the rest of the District's fleet and remained isolated as a batch until its withdrawal in 1963, by which time it had been operating on the Metropolitan Line for some ten years.

By the time the F Stock entered service in 1921, a rescue plan had been formulated for the wooden stock. The worst of the trailers were to be scrapped and the remainder refurbished. The scrapped cars were to be replaced by converting wooden motor cars to trailers. The steel strengthening had left them in much better condition than the trailers. The gap left by the conversion of the motor cars was to be filled by new motor cars using the electrical equipment from the converted cars. This plan, which opted for the cheaper patching up of the old stock instead of its replacement by new cars of the F Stock standard was to have a profound effect on the development of rolling stock on the District. It guaranteed the survival of the American style, with its clerestory roof, for many years and it prolonged the operation of incompatible batches of stock on the line.

A total of 150 wooden motor cars were converted to trailers and classified as H Stock over the next five years and were replaced by two batches of new steel motor cars, the G and K Stocks. These were ordered in 1923 and 1927 respectively. They reverted to the clerestory-roofed design of pre-1914 stocks, presumably because they were to run with them. Many of them survived until the end of clerestory stock on the District in 1971.

Towards the end of the conversion programme, it was decided to re-equip all the steel cars with new traction equipment. This meant that, following the completion of the delivery of the K Stock and the conversion of older cars in 1930, the District had three different types of stock: the F Stock, the steel and converted stock and the remainder of the wooden stock, still with its original equipment, now down to fewer than 60 cars and confined to working the 'local' services on the Putney, Hounslow and Rayners Lane branches.

# A Balancing Act

With the end of the first world war, the Underground took the opportunity to use Government assisted finance to expand its market and improve existing services. It was particularly interested in improving services from west London. The five branches from Hounslow, Ealing, Uxbridge, Richmond and Wimbledon all funnelled traffic through Earl's Court towards the City. Train working through the junctions became very difficult at peak times, a small delay to one train quickly impacting upon the rest of the service. Some relief was achieved in 1914 when a diveunder was opened at the west end of Earl's Court to remove conflicts between westbound trains to Hammersmith and eastbound trains from Putney.

There was also a high level of interchange traffic at Hammersmith between the District and the Piccadilly tube terminus. A scheme was therefore developed to extend the Piccadilly Line westwards to take over some District workings. This had the dual attraction of improving the variety of routes available for passengers and of easing the pressure of train working through Earl's Court. It was also proposed to balance the reduction of District services at the western end of the line by expanding services in the east.

The first plans had been drafted in 1912 and envisaged the Piccadilly Line being extended to Richmond and Hounslow. They also envisaged extension of electrification of the LT&S line from Barking to Upminster. When it was delivered in 1921, the F Stock was fitted with indicators which proposed non-stopping stations as far east as Hornchurch and some prototype tube cars were ordered with interior maps showing the western extensions. However, the scheme was shelved in 1922 in favour of improving the City & South London Railway and extending the Hampstead tube north to Edgware and south to Morden to form what is now the Northern Line.

The large amount of extra stock required for the extension of the Northern Line and the expansion of services on other lines, including the District, led to increased demands on depot space. Ealing Common Depot had, during the early years of electric operation, taken in Piccadilly stock for overhauls as well as its own but it became so overcrowded after the steel stock deliveries between 1910 and 1914 that new premises were sought. Eventually, Acton Works was built to the south of the main line at Acton Town with the express purpose of providing long term overhaul facilities for District and tube cars while day-to-day maintenance continued to be done at depots. The first part of the new works was opened in 1922 and it was extended in stages up to the beginning of the second world war in 1939.

In the meantime, there were limited improvements to the District in the west. The Hounslow line saw a big increase in housing development during the early 1920s and improvements to the unusual arrangements at the western end of the line were gradually put in place. The original line to Hounslow Town station had been closed in 1886 but was reopened from 1st March 1903. The line was converted to electric traction on 13th June 1905 and trains worked from South Acton to Hounslow Barracks via Hounslow Town where they reversed. A new connecting line was opened to connect Hounslow Town to Heston-Hounslow. The direct line to the Barracks fell into disuse.

# UNDERGROUND

E.L.BAMFORD.

# WIMBLEDON
## BY DISTRICT RLY

"And little footpaths sweet to see
Go seeking sweeter places still"

Hounslow Town was finally closed on 1st May 1909 and a new station of the same name opened on 2nd May 1909 on the line to Hounslow Barracks. This became Hounslow East on 1st December 1925. The line to the Barracks station was single until 1910 when work on doubling it began. It was doubled as far as Heston-Hounslow (renamed Hounslow Central on 1st December 1925) on 1st November 1912 and was finally doubled to the Barracks on 27th November 1926.

The 1920s also saw the beginnings of what was to become a serious competitor to the railway. The Great West Road was opened in 1928, paralleling the District from Chiswick to Hounslow. Although it helped to develop the area and spawned the building of many factories and small industries, it was eventually to be the cause of a contraction in the levels of train services which could economically be provided. As the popularity of private car ownership grew it came into direct competition with the District, particularly for off-peak travel.

Plans for wider-scale improvements in the west were to wait for ten years before becoming reality. When more Government assisted finance became available in 1929, the Underground reviewed its plans for the west. The Piccadilly Line was to take over the District services to South Harrow and Uxbridge and was to provide some services to Hounslow. To implement this scheme, the line west of Turnham Green was quadrupled as far as Northfields where a large depot was built to house both District and Piccadilly trains. West of Barons Court, the tracks were rearranged so that the Piccadilly Line used the centre tracks and the District the outer tracks. This gave better cross platform interchange at Barons Court and Hammersmith. At Hammersmith the station was rebuilt in stages; at one time the Piccadilly service having to reverse in one terminal platform while the other track was used by eastbound District trains. New stations were also built at Chiswick Park, which had platforms serving only the District tracks, and at Acton Town, which now had two island platforms for the through services and a short platform for the South Acton service.

Many of the stations on the Hounslow and Rayners Lane branches were rebuilt to the designs of Charles Holden in the modern style of the early 1930s and are now regarded as classics of twentieth century design. One which survived in its original form was North Ealing. It remains today as it was built in 1903, complete with a flat over the station which was originally occupied by the District Inspector and whose telephone was connected to the railway network.

As part of the reconstruction, the largely disused connection to Addison Road just east of Ravenscourt Park was disconnected. The Southern Railway (now the owners of the L&SWR) gave up their interest in their remaining tracks from there to the junction at Gunnersbury Lane and their staff were replaced by Underground staff. To serve the new eastbound District track at Stamford Brook, a new platform was built opposite the original island platform station. The former eastbound District platform face is now passed by westbound Piccadilly trains. There is no eastbound Piccadilly platform.

Piccadilly trains first began running west of Hammersmith to South Harrow in July 1932, to Uxbridge in October 1933 and to Hounslow in March 1933. The branch to South Acton was singled and converted to a shuttle service to Acton Town. A single car operated only by a driver was specially converted for this service and it was the first instance of one person operation on the Underground. A new depot for District and Piccadilly trains was built at Northfields and opened in 1932 and, from that time until District trains ceased using Northfields Depot in 1964, some Piccadilly trains were stabled at Ealing Common.

**Hornchurch on the extension to Upminster opened over the route of the LMS in 1932. The line remained in LMS and, later, BR ownership until 1969.** LT Museum

The loss of District services on the western side of London was balanced by improvements in the east. As planned ten years earlier, the eastern end of the District was extended to Upminster. The line between Barking and Upminster was provided with two additional tracks by the London Midland & Scottish Railway (who now owned the line) and these were electrified for use by District trains. The new facilities, came into operation on 12th September 1932. Additional stations were opened at Upminster Bridge in 1934 and at Elm Park in 1935.

Some of the trains for the extended services were provided by those released by the opening of the Piccadilly extensions into District territory in the west but some 45 new cars were also ordered. These were similar to the earlier clerestory-roofed types and were designated L Stock.

The ownership of some of these cars was vested in the LMS. This carried on the arrangement first started in 1901 with the delivery of the new stock for the Whitechapel and Bow Railway, when half of the six trains were owned by the District and half by the LT&S. When the line was electrified in 1905, a proportion of the District's B Stock displayed 'L T & S RAILWAY' instead of 'DISTRICT RAILWAY' over the side windows, in recognition of its ownership.

A guard of a westbound Ealing train at Earl's Court gives the driver the starting signal. The tip of his flag has a brass ferrule which, when placed against two bare copper wires, rings a bell at the driver's end of the platform. This system, introduced in the 1920s, lasted until the end of hand-worked door stock in 1959. LT Museum

# London Transport

In July 1933 the ownership of the Underground railways, tramways and bus companies in the London region was transferred to the London Passenger Transport Board. From that time and for over 40 years, London Transport appeared on the sides of the board's road and rail vehicles and soon became the name known to millions of Londoners as the organisation responsible for the Underground and road services.

The new organisation saw the start of a 1935-40 New Works Programme to revitalise the existing system and expand into potential new suburbs. Much had already been done for the east-west axis of the District so the bulk of the work was concentrated on the Northern and Central Lines.

There was a complex rebuilding scheme at Aldgate East. The existing station was cramped, with only one exit, and it was positioned close to the junction of the District and Metropolitan Lines where the tracks from Liverpool Street and Tower Hill converged. The third side of a triangle was formed by the Inner Circle connection from Tower Hill and Liverpool Street via Aldgate. The triangle was so small that it was impossible for a full-length train to stand on some of the lines without fouling the junctions at either end. This was the cause of many delays at peak times, so it was decided to rebuild Aldgate East station and move it almost 200ft eastwards.

The work was carried out in stages using weekend changeovers to enlarge the eastern tunnel, move sewers and install cross girders, lowering the tracks and building the new station. The new layout was brought into use in November 1938, allowing 8-car trains to stand on the legs of the triangle without fouling the junctions.

**The rebuilt and resited station at Aldgate East, brought into use in 1938.**
LT Museum

By the mid-1930s the District still had over 200 wooden cars which were due for replacement, but there was some doubt as to how this should actually be done while the plans for integrating the surface lines were being considered. Various schemes were proposed, including services which started on a branch, say at Uxbridge, and then proceeded via Baker Street, round the Circle via Tower Hill and then to Wimbledon. The diversity of stock then in use, the difficulty of training all the crews to work over all the lines and the risk to reliability and recovery programmes stopped the idea, but some District stock was used on the Metropolitan Line for a time during 1938-40 to see how integration might work.

During this period some additional stock was built to the L Stock design of 1931. Two batches, the M Stock, consisting of 14 motor cars and 14 trailers, and the N Stock (26 trailers) were ordered in 1935. The M Stock, consisting of two 6-car trains and two spare cars was introduced on the Hammersmith & City Line in 1936. One of the trains had a trial system of passenger push-button door control. The other new cars retained the handworked door system.

Passenger door control was designed in response to passenger requests to find some way of keeping trains warm during cold weather. Many trains at open stations did not require all doors to be opened. The unnecessary opening led to heat loss and passenger discomfort. The trial was successful enough for the equipment to be included in the order for new stock in 1938 but it was withdrawn during the 1939-45 war. It was gradually reintroduced on the District during the early 1950s but was withdrawn again in March 1959, as it was technically difficult to maintain. It was always the intention to find a way of reintroducing it one day and it finally became possible when the District introduced its present stock in 1980.

Opposite **Wood and steel bodied motor car of C stock, built in 1910, seen at High Street Kensington later in life.** F.G. Reynolds

Above **Eastbound District train approaching Gloucester Road in May 1935 over the double junction with the 'Cromwell Curve'. On the right are the Car Sheds used by the District until their removal in 1957 prior to the construction of the West London Air Terminal at this location.** LT Museum

By 1938, the first of the District's replacement cars began to arrive. They were of a very modern design for the time, having a smooth all-steel body incorporating a flared 'skirt' at floor level. They entered service as direct replacements for the old wooden cars and were placed into trains having clerestoried motor cars. As they had air operated doors, the older motor cars were converted to match.

The new cars were known as Q stock and had bodies identical to those of the new stock introduced on the Metropolitan and Hammersmith & City Lines from 1936-37. It was the original intention that all the new bodies would eventually be equipped as driving motor cars and have a new traction control system incorporating regenerative braking and using a machine called a Metadyne. Metadyne equipment had been fitted to the new Metropolitan stock but the new District cars had traditional resistance control to enable them to work with older District cars. Of the 208 Q Stock cars built for the District, all had dummy driving cab doors fitted at one end but only 25 were delivered as motor cars; the rest were run as trailers.

The motor cars converted to air doors to run with the Q Stock became Q Converted Stock. The F Stock was also converted to air doors as part of the New Works

**Q Stock was made up of cars of no fewer than five different types, dating from 1923, 1927, 1931, 1935 and 1938. The 1938-built ones were of similar design to the O and P Stocks of the same vintage and their flared sides created trains of most odd appearance. S.L. Poole**

Programme. The remaining stock, comprising cars built between 1910 and 1935, retained its hand-operated doors pending the replacement of the 1910-14 cars in the group.

The inclusion of all the surface lines under one management had, as mentioned above, led to proposals to offer passengers better services by combining the routes of the Metropolitan, District and Circle lines. Many variations were put forward but eventually a Barking to Uxbridge service was introduced in 1938 using Metropolitan stock. A Hammersmith (Metropolitan) service to Barking had started in 1935 using a combination of Metropolitan and District trains and some services on the Metropolitan main line also began using District trains in 1938 on its Rayners Lane to Barking service to test passenger reaction and to maintain the stock balance. Ultimately the second world war intervened to stop such experiments but it was already becoming apparent that such diverse combinations made it almost impossible to recover from any delays. Indeed, the knock-on effect of a delay anywhere on the sub-surface lines of the system left all services in chaos. The only survivor of these ideas is the present day service between Barking and Hammersmith (H&C line).

**The interior of a 1938 built Q Stock trailer. The box by the left hand doorway contained destination plates which were carried on the exterior of the car sides.** LT Museum

# The Second World War and After

The replacement of the last of the District wooden rolling stock was already well under way by the time the second world war started in September 1939. The original declaration of war did not prevent the continuation of the rolling stock replacement programme and it was not until 1941 that the bulk of the work was completed. By that time the District Line had 183 new steel bodied trailer cars and 25 new motor cars. As already mentioned, these were incorporated into the Q stock, operating with older motor cars whose door equipment had been converted to air operation and which were known as Q Converted stock.

**Air raid damage
at Plaistow,
7th September 1940,
with East Ham depot
just visible in the
background.**
LT Museum U31749

From September 1940, London was the target of repeated bombing attacks and the District, being more exposed than the deep level tube lines, often suffered severe damage to trains, tracks and stations. A total of 11 cars of District stock were lost during the war. An example of how the railway was affected by air raids was demonstrated by one of the earliest attacks to affect the District. There was particularly severe damage at Plaistow on 7th September 1940, where one car was blown on to the top of another and had to be cut up on site in order to remove it. Five other trains were stalled by the incident but the desire to get the service going again as quickly as possible meant that the work of removing the debris was carried out while bombs were still falling. Repairs were finished in time for the through service to be started within 24 hours.

Whitechapel was a common victim as both the station and sub-station were frequently hit by bombs, sometimes putting them out of action for days at a time. St James's Park station was also hit, as was the District Line Depot at East Ham where, on one particular raid, 70 vehicles were damaged by a land mine.

One of the worst incidents was at Sloane Square during the winter of 1940. At 10pm one night, as a train was just leaving the station, a bomb fell and caused a large lump of concrete to fall through the roof of one of the cars. There were 79 casualties. Work on rebuilding the station had only been completed six months previously and it had to be rebuilt again after the war. There was also a particularly bad night on 10th May 1941. The section between St James's Park and Victoria was closed when feeder cables were severed in the tunnel. There was an unexploded bomb outside Victoria station which required it to be closed for seven days and debris on the track stopped the service through Sloane Square. There was further damage at Stepney Green and the service was suspended between Bow Road and Whitechapel for the next two days. In some cases the service had to be suspended for several weeks due to damage to the tunnels.

**Air Raid damage at Sloane Square, November 1940. The wreckage includes that of the escalators, installed when the station was rebuilt eight months earlier.** LT Museum U32245

Although there was a lull in 1943, during 1944 and 1945 the District again suffered as a result of attacks by the famous V1 flying bombs and V2 rockets. East Ham Depot was again damaged in one of those incidents and the District Line services were regularly suspended during these periods because of bomb damage. When the war ended in 1945 work began immediately on reviewing what needed to be done to return services to normal. For the District Line there were several plans to improve services. These included the introduction of better signalling, the replacement of the remaining pre-first world war rolling stock and the lengthening of platforms to allow 8-car trains to operate without restriction. Shortage of money and materials prevented much of this work taking place immediately but it was phased in over the next few years. One outstanding job was the repair of the station at Sloane Square. Money was short so it was not until 1951 that a new prefabricated entrance and platform canopies were provided.

**Whitechapel's proximity to the London docks meant that it suffered more than most from air raids, though the London Transport electrical sub station here may also have been a target. This attack was in March 1941.** LT Museum U32777

After the war, further new rolling stock was introduced on the District. The plan was to replace stock built before the first world war which had reached its life-expiry age of 35 years. This included the Metropolitan's Circle Line trains and some of the District's C, D & E Stocks built between 1910 and 1914. The Circle Line loomed large in the deliberations because its stock was giving a lot of trouble. There were a number of cases of cracked bogie frames, collapsed wheel centres and defective door gear. Some wheel sets and bogies were replaced by spares removed from scrapped wooden District cars but there were not enough of them to re-equip the whole stock of 90 cars and anyway hand-worked doors were regarded as obsolete.

There was a considerable body of opinion in favour of replacing the Circle stock before the old District stock, but it was decided that the Circle stock would be replaced, not by new trains but by 18 x 5-car trains of P Stock removed from the Metropolitan Line's Uxbridge service. The gap thus created would be filled by trains of F Stock transferred from the District. The removal of the F Stock from the District was to be covered by the purchase of new cars to be known as R Stock. This cascade programme allowed the withdrawal of the unreliable Circle fleet and the use of the powerful F Stock on the higher speed Metropolitan Line. However, it still left some pre-first world war cars on the District.

The arrival of the new cars was to be accompanied by the conversion of some of the 1938 built Q stock trailers to new driving cars to work with the new stock being delivered. The provision of dummy cab doors at one end of the cars made the conversion easier. The new trains were to be marshalled into 6- or 8-car formations as was then standard on the District. All the cars were to be motor cars, with those at the ends of the train having driving cabs and the others being called non-driving motors. The Q cars to be converted to run with them were to be those at the ends with the driving cabs. These cars would be known as R38 Stock whilst the non driving motors would be classified R47 Stock. There was to be a total of 31 trains, the work beginning in November 1949. The first 8-car train entered service on 17th April 1950.

Opposite
**A converted R38 motor car, formerly a Q38 trailer, leading an R Stock train at West Brompton. When built, the R Stock had shoegear without shoebeams. It was equipped with shoebeams during the early 1960s.**
F.G. Reynolds

Left **Interior of a 1949-built R Stock car.** LT Museum

The R Stock also saw the introduction of fluorescent lighting on an Underground fleet for the first time. Some experiments had been conducted on a few Underground cars immediately after the war and the improvement to lighting levels was a popular enhancement after the years of reduced lighting during the wartime blackout.

The R47 Stock order of 31 trains was not sufficient to provide enough new stock for the District Line and, as was originally intended, the East London Line. Nor did it allow all the 1910 to 1914 cars on the District to be replaced. The shortage of steel in particular was one of the reasons why only 31 trains were ordered. A further 90 cars were therefore ordered in 1949, to be known as the R49 Stock. These would allow the replacement of majority of the old C, D & E Stock.

One of the reasons why it had become possible to order the remaining cars required for the District, was the introduction of aluminium technology to railway car building. Aluminium technology had been accelerated by the needs of the aircraft industry during the second world war and the possibilities of using aluminium to replace steel for railway cars was seen as a much needed way of reducing the country's requirements for steel.

The aluminium underframe and skin construction introduced on the R49 Stock was to become a feature which was to be a hallmark of London Transport design excellence for many years. However, the use of aluminium in car body construction on the Underground was not new. The 1905 built B Stock cars had aluminium body side sheets screwed onto wooden framing to provide additional strength as well as a smooth surface finish, and aluminium castings were common for such items as sliding doors and ventilator grilles, particularly after the first world war.

Another advantage was that with an overall saving of over 16% on each aluminium car body there was considerable scope for energy saving. As post-war fuel costs increased, the early adverse financial balance against aluminium construction, which was very costly in its early days, gradually shifted and aluminium construction became standard on London Underground and, later, widespread throughout the world.

One advantage of the aluminium body was its resistance to corrosion. In order to protect the traditional mild steel body, various coats of primer, undercoat, body colour and finishing varnish had to be applied to each car to ensure maximum resistance to rust and to give a reasonable appearance. The introduction of aluminium construction on the R Stock prompted an experiment with an unpainted exterior finish on a car. One of the R49 cars, No.23567 was therefore delivered unpainted in April 1952 and entered service on 12th June. Its technical excellence and its rapid acceptance by the travelling public prompted the Underground to authorise the running of complete 8-car trains of unpainted cars. The first of these arrived in October 1952. From this time all cars built for the London Underground were delivered with unpainted aluminium exteriors. Only since 1984, with the incidence of graffiti, has the need to protect the car body finish from damage with specially resistant paint seen the return of a coloured exterior to London Underground trains.

The first unpainted R Stock car for the District was the subject of much interest in the engineering world and unpainted District Line cars were shown at the South Bank Exhibition in 1951, the International Railway Congress Exhibition in 1954 and an aluminium development exhibition in June 1955, also held on the South Bank. Another exhibition took place in 1960 in Strasbourg where District car number 23584 was shipped for display.

In 1959 a final batch of R59 Stock was delivered to replace the oldest of the C, D and E Stocks dating from before the first world war. The 20 new vehicles (one 8-car and two 6-car trains) were compatible with the original R Stock fleet of 1947 and 1949 except they were all aluminium and unpainted, meeting the new standard adopted for the whole of the Underground for new trains from that time.

Plans for improving the services over the lines east of London were implemented over the former LT&S line from 1953 when work began on electrifying the line to Tilbury and Shoeburyness. By this time the line was vested in the Eastern Region of British Railways, having been transferred from the London Midland Region in February 1949. As the line was to be converted to the 25kV overhead line system, it was considered desirable to segregate the District and BR services. From July 1955 the power supply for the District services was vested in London Transport. The station at Barking was completely rebuilt with two flyovers and a flyunder to segregate the Underground tracks and platforms. The new station was opened on 29th September 1961.

The District depot at East Ham was closed in December 1958 following the opening of a new depot at Upminster. The East Ham site was needed for a new electric train depot for the LT&S stock.

The District tracks were resignalled over the period between October 1959 and November 1960 and control transferred to new signal boxes at Barking and Upminster. In spite of all the segregation work being completed by the end of 1961, it was not until 1st January 1969 that London Transport actually took over the lines and stations (excluding Barking and Upminster, which remained in BR ownership).

The rolling stock was not the only part of the District to get substantial improvements following the second world war. Much of the signalling on the District Line was still operating under the same principles as under the original electrification schemes and, west of Hammersmith, there was still some automatic signalling using semaphore arms in place. During the late 1940s and early 1950s, much of this was replaced by colour light signals.

**The experimental unpainted R49 Stock car No.23567 in a train of red painted cars.**
F.G. Reynolds

**Two complete trains of unpainted R Stock were delivered in 1953. One is seen here working the Olympia service.** Photomatic

Further improvements to the signalling on the District were undertaken during the mid-1950s with an installation of what was known as speed control signalling. One of the critical points of running a close headway intensive suburban service like the Underground is the delay caused by station stops. The train following will be delayed if the train in the platform does not leave quickly after station work. To reduce the possibility of the following train coming to a stand, it became the practice to introduce several home signals. This would allow a following train to re-start sooner than had been the case if there were only one home signal at the full safe braking distance away from the platform. The additional home signals cleared in sequence as the departing train left the station allowing the following train to run in close behind it.

A refinement of this multi-home signalling system was known as speed control. The number of signals was increased to six and the first two signals were provided with a device to allow them to clear provided the driver had reduced the train's speed sufficiently to maintain a safe braking distance from the train in the platform. The speed was measured by the passage of the train as it approached the signal and, if the speed was low enough, usually 25 mph, the first signal was cleared. If it had fallen to 20 mph by the second signal this would also clear. By that time, the preceding train should already have been leaving the station allowing the following four signals to clear successively as it departed.

This system had been tried on the tube lines during the late 1940s using a track circuit actuated time element relay. For the District Line system, which was installed between Sloane Square and Mansion House, a dummy conductor rail with speed detection coils was provided as the monitoring device. It was described as an instantaneous inductive speed detector. It was to prove valuable in saving a few seconds of delay for each train approaching a congested station.

The speed control signalling system gave valuable service for over 20 years but it was gradually removed during the 1970s because of its maintenance costs and, with the fall in train service levels, it meant that it was less useful than before.

The District was also to see a pioneer installation of route-setting signal cabin frames. The first such installation was opened at Ealing Broadway in 1952. The system was based on the idea that electrical signals would be sent from the signal lever or switch in the cabin to a frame carrying all the required mechanical interlocking at a remote installation. The success of the installation at Ealing Broadway led to its widespread adoption throughout the Underground and to the idea that, eventually, the train descriptions used to display information to passengers on platforms could actually control the setting up of the routes for the trains.

In 1955 some trials were carried out on the Northern Line with what was referred to as a programme machine. The programme machine is an electromechanical device which carries the details of the day's train service in the form of a roll of plastic film eight inches wide with holes punched in a line across it to provide the route and identification information for each train. With a maximum length of about 40ft, sufficient information for about 1200 trains can be accommodated. The information is sent to the interlocking room near the area to be controlled by electrical signals transmitted from the programme machine.

The programme roll is driven round to the next train by a small electric motor until photocells are lined up through the positioning holes to stop it in the correct position. The reading of the train identification and route information is through holes which connect a series of feelers acting as switches. When the contacts are closed, circuits are set up for the operation of the routes through the junctions concerned.

**Semaphore signalling at the Hammersmith end of Barons Court platform in the 1950s.**
LT Museum 52768

Following the introduction of programme machines on the Northern Line, with installations at Euston, Finchley, Morden and Tooting, much of the line was controlled from a regulating room at Leicester Square. Its success led to a similar scheme being introduced for the District.

Installations on the District Line began in 1961 at Earl's Court and continued as far east as Tower Hill and as far west as Ealing. A central control room was established at Earl's Court and enabled the closure of a number of signal cabins along the line. Whilst the programme machines have served the railway well for over 30 years, they are now becoming old and new parts will be difficult to obtain. It is hoped that in the next few years it will be possible to replace this control system by an up-to-date computer-based system which will allow much more flexible operation of the service and a better response to aid recovery from delays. Coupled with this, new passenger information systems could be provided which will be based on real-time information generated by the computers tracking the course of the trains through the line.

Accurate passenger information has always been considered paramount by the Underground and the pioneer installation of platform train indicators produced in 1905 for the original District Line electrification formed the basis for the rest of the London Underground. Many of the inner city stations on the District now have new dot matrix type indicators but, as these are driven by the old programme machines, it is not possible to provide better information until the machines are replaced.

The period between 1959 and 1964 saw a rationalisation of District services to cope with changes in passenger demand. The under-used South Acton shuttle to Acton Town was withdrawn on 2nd March 1959 and the line closed. From 10th October 1964 District services between Acton Town and Hounslow were withdrawn, the whole service being provided by the Piccadilly Line. From that time, District trains no longer used Northfields Depot and Piccadilly trains were no longer stabled in Ealing Common Depot. From the same time, non-stop trains were withdrawn over all District routes.

A short branch of the District Line had been created in 1932 when the service to South Acton was cut back to start from Acton Town instead of Hounslow. This branch lasted until 1959. It was always very lightly used but boasted its own booking office next to that of the LMS, seen in this 1950 photograph.

From 1932 until closure of the branch, the South Acton service was normally a single car shuttle working from Acton Town. Sometimes the single car was replaced by a 2-car train as seen here at the special South Acton shuttle platform at Acton Town. Photomatic

From the time of the electrification of the District Line in 1905, there had been a restriction on the length of trains which could be used along the central section of the line between South Kensington and Tower Hill. This restriction was due to the length of station platforms which were, in many cases, 300ft. This meant that the original 7-car formation adopted for the electrification could not be completely accommodated in these platforms. This problem became worse from 1908 when 8-car trains began to appear. In order to accommodate these longer trains the District had negotiated with the Board of Trade that they could build narrow cat-walks at the platform ends to accommodate the 8-car trains. These cat-walks were generally 2ft or 2ft 6in in width and use of them had to be closely supervised by the guard at the end of the train. Even so, there were still some places where the last pair of doors could not be used because there was insufficient room to install a cat-walk.

At the end of the second world war the capacity of the District Line was stretched to its limits. The delays which still occurred to trains while passengers negotiated the cat-walks were a restriction on the performance of the service. It was therefore proposed to lengthen platforms wherever this was possible and work began in earnest in 1955 at Monument.

The tunnel at this end of the station had already been damaged by a bomb explosion during the war, and before re-building the Westminster Bank premises over the track the opportunity was taken to widen the tunnel for 70ft eastwards to accommodate the platform extensions. During the work it was necessary for the workmen to occupy a strong room in the basement in an adjacent branch of Lloyds Bank. The bank were very nervous about this and insisted that their officials were on site at all times while the work was being done. Many of them had to spend long nights guarding the room while the engineers worked during the non-traffic hours to do the work affecting the railway itself.

The next station to be tackled was Blackfriars. This work was very difficult because it involved the demolition of the existing running tunnel and the construction of a wide covered way under the road between Blackfriars Bridge and Queen Victoria Street. The work also involved bridging the river Fleet, one of the rivers of London which was once a navigable waterway, but which is now reduced to a sewer.

**Extended platforms at Blackfriars, 1962.** LT Museum 440/831

**Upminster depot was opened in 1958 to replace the depot at East Ham and to take over some of the responsibilities of Ealing Common depot.** LT Museum

When Westminster station was tackled in 1962 again the eastern end was chosen for the extension. This however involved extensive works supporting the original Police headquarters building known as Scotland Yard. The load placed on the underpinning of the building was about 800 tons. Some very careful measurements had to be taken during the underpinning work to ensure that neither the building nor the tunnel walls moved in a way that was likely to become dangerous. The work was completed in 1964. It is ironic to note that only a few years later the Police headquarters was transferred to a new building almost directly opposite the London Underground Headquarters at 55 Broadway, although the original building still exists.

Cannon Street was reconstructed as part of a development planned over the Southern Region's main line station at the same point. There was also a City Corporation road widening scheme which gave the financial backing for the District station to be modernised and lengthened. Much of the work on this site also involved the use of Bailey Bridges to ensure that traffic could still use the streets above.

During the 1950s, South Kensington was considerably altered. Formerly, the station had always been in two parts, the platforms on the north side belonging to the Metropolitan and the platforms on the south side to the District. The Metropolitan had a bay road approached from the west between the two double tracks while the District had a siding which was accessed from the eastern end of the station and was used very rarely. A re-arrangement of the tracks between Gloucester Road and South Kensington in 1957 converted the Metropolitan platforms at both stations to be two eastbound lines and the District platforms to become two westbound lines. This allowed some trains to non-stop the stations during peak times. The former Met bay road at South Kensington was removed and subsequently became part of a wide island platform. Between 1971 and 1973, the station was altered again to allow escalators to be installed between the Piccadilly and District Lines and these works also saw the lengthening of platforms to take a full 8-car train. The outer tracks were removed leaving just one eastbound and one westbound track on either side of the island platform. Non-stopping had ceased on the District in 1964.

**The start of work at Cromwell Curve on the construction overhead of the West London Air Terminal.** LT Museum U58620

The last major work on the platform extension project was the rebuilding of Tower Hill station. Traffic east of the City turnround point at Mansion House had risen steadily since the war and it was decided that the opportunity should be taken to provide a new terminus further east. Reconstruction of the station also allowed a new site closer to the BR station at Fenchurch Street station providing better interchange for passengers with the London, Tilbury and Southend Line. The site of the new Tower Hill Station was where the original Metropolitan Railway Tower Hill station had been built as a temporary terminus and which was closed in 1884 after Mark Lane Station was opened. Mark Lane was renamed Tower Hill on 1st September 1946.

The new Tower Hill station was opened on 5th February 1967 and the old station closed the same day. As part of this reconstruction project it was necessary to considerably widen the tracks at the site of the new station. The former westbound road thus became the centre terminating and reversing road and a new westbound track with a widened platform was built on the south side of this.

In addition to improving services by increasing the reversing facilities on the line, opportunities have been taken to use the space occupied by the railway to encourage development by property companies. One more recent example was the provision of an air terminal over the triangular area bounded by the District and Circle Lines at High Street Kensington. From here, a fleet of express buses provided a link to Heathrow Airport. The building of the terminal necessitated the removal of the two additional tracks between Gloucester Road and High Street Kensington known as the Cromwell Curve. Some sidings were also dispensed with. The work was completed in 1961. Today the site is occupied by a Sainsbury's Supermarket.

At Knaresborough Place between Gloucester Road and Earl's Court stations, a further development took place during the late 1960s. This involved reconstructing the bridges and rafting over the tracks to allow the construction of a hotel. Since that time developments have also been carried out at Monument, Mansion House, Gloucester Road and High Street Kensington and a further development is proposed over the station at South Kensington.

Preparation for the building of London's first completely new tube line (the Victoria Line) since before the first world war included a number of experiments with new systems of railway operation. One of these was automatic train operation (ATO) which was tested on the District Line during the early 1960s.

The operation of a train equipped with automatic acceleration and retarder controlled braking can, within quite close limits, be precisely predicted. Most London Underground trains had these features by the mid-1950s and so, in 1955, some tentative suggestions were made that automatic control of trains was a practical proposition. At the time it was suggested that suitable places to carry out practical tests would be the single line branches between Acton Town and South Acton or Holborn and Aldwych. Both of these, however, would have involved a high level of technology for a limited service and with limited scope. It was decided therefore, to carry out the initial trials on the eastbound Piccadilly Line 'test track' between South Ealing and Acton Town, and then do a trial on a service train.

The principles of Automatic Train Operation (ATO) are quite simple. Motoring is activated by closing a switch and braking is activated by opening that switch and closing another. The only real complication is in the precise positioning of a train in a station platform. By May 1958 sufficient work had been done on the safety aspects of ATO to convince the Ministry of Transport that LT should be allowed to start trials. Almost two years later, in March 1961, it had been arranged to equip a 2-car east end unit of District Line R stock (23580-22681) with the necessary equipment.

To transmit the signals from the track to the train so that the train would know the state of the line ahead and know where to stop at a station, a pair of induction coils was mounted on each side of the leading bogie of 22681. The coils picked up coded signals from the track which gave the safety indications plus the braking commands for signal and station stops.

The test train was also equipped with a radio for communication between the cab and the test engineers' hut at South Ealing.

Test running began on 3rd December 1962 and a rapid build-up of confidence in the system persuaded the test team to show it off to the Vice-Chairman, Anthony Bull, on 25th January 1963. The success of this demonstration led to the authorisation of the next step in the scheme — a full scale trial of an ATO passenger train. The eastbound District Line between Stamford Brook and Ravenscourt Park was chosen for the trial and, after the press were given a demonstration run at South Ealing on 21st March, the date for the first day of public running was announced for 8th April.

The equipment for the public trial was taken off 22681 and fitted to 22682 between 27th March and 4th April. The signalling between Stamford Brook and Ravenscourt Park was connected up to ATO on the night of Saturday/Sunday 6th/7th April and a series of trials with a 6-car train (22682 leading) took place on the Sunday morning. The MoT carried out an inspection in the afternoon. The inspectors were satisfied and the first public run took place on the morning of the 8th April in the working of train No.123.

The trial was arranged so that train No.123 was made up with 22682 leading each weekday morning and, when it arrived at Stamford Brook, the driver closed a special automatic control master switch. When he wanted to start the train, he pulled and then pushed a special double-action starting button. The double action was to prevent inadvertent operation.

The starting button could show a white, blue or yellow light to indicate that the code being received from the track was 'high', 'medium', or 'low' respectively, according

The first trials of Automatic Train Operation in Britain were carried out on the District. The test train is seen here on the test track between Acton Town and South Ealing in December 1963. This development work allowed ATO to be introduced on the new Victoria Line in 1968.
LT Museum 3033/R5

to the state of the line ahead. The white allowed full speed running, the blue allowed controlled speed running at about 20mph while the yellow gave a signal-stop brake command.

At Ravenscourt Park, the train would stop at the 6-car stopping mark where a special yellow marker board was provided. Here, the driver switched out the automatic control and carried on the trip in manual as normal. Between April 1963 and April 1964, a considerable number of trips were made by the automatic train. On occasions, the unit was withdrawn for alterations to the equipment, decided upon as a result of the service experience, or for test train runs over the South Ealing to Acton Town section.

During the summer of 1963, as a result of the success of these trials, it was decided to convert some units of 1960 tube stock and go ahead with a full-scale trial on the Woodford-Hainault section of the Central Line. The new Victoria Line, which was finally authorised in 1962, was also to get the system. When No.22682 was sent to Acton Works for overhaul in April 1964, its automatic equipment was removed and the car converted back to normal.

Although ATO was installed on the Victoria Line, it was never possible to adopt it throughout the rest of the system unless the opportunity to renew signalling and rolling stock occurred at the same time (as has happened on the Central Line). In the meantime, one-person operation has been adopted as a means of improving efficiency. The first lines to go over to OPO were the Circle and Hammersmith Lines in March 1984 and the District followed in November 1985.

Another new scheme planned for the Victoria Line was automatic fare collection (AFC). The District Line was again the scene for a number of trials. An automatic ticket barrier was installed at Stamford Brook on 5th January 1964 and further large scale trials were started at Hammersmith from 19th March 1969. These trials were to show that AFC was not to be as easy to introduce as first thought and it was to be many years before a satisfactory system was available for the Underground. Following experiments at Vauxhall in 1983, it was 1987 before full-scale installation began at Hammersmith (Metropolitan) station.

# A Period of Transformation

In the 1960s the District Line was still running a fleet of rolling stock consisting of three different and incompatible types. The oldest was the Q Stock which consisted of cars of various ages built between 1923 and 1938. It was a legacy of the 1935-40 new works programme which had sought to combine the fleets of varying ages to make up a fleet of air worked door trains. The second batch of cars was known as the CO/CP Stock (converted O and P Stock).

Until 1962, there had been no official allocation of the CO/CP Stock on the District except during the period 1937 to 1942, when trains were allocated to the District to work the services left vacant by the transfer of Q Stock to the Metropolitan Line during the experiments with combining services of both lines. The CO/CP only came to the District in large numbers from 1962 at the start of a programme of removing the oldest of the Q Stock. Between that time and the withdrawal of the Q Stock in 1971 this stock worked on the District with the Q Stock and the R Stock.

A further rolling stock development took place in the summer of 1971 to remove the anomalies caused by the practice of uncoupling on the District, which enabled short trains to run in off-peak hours. There were difficulties after a disruption of the service when trying to ensure that the correct type of stock was able to couple at the correct location. There was also the need to have staff available to reform trains to 8-car lengths for peak periods. A scheme was begun of converting all the CO, CP and R Stock trains to 7-car length, except for those operating the Edgware Road services. The latter had platforms capable of accommodating 6-car trains only.

**CP Stock train approaching Wimbledon in April 1964.** J.P. Mullett, courtesy Colour-Rail

**A mixed train of Q Stock leaving Plaistow for Wimbledon in April 1959. The leading motor car is of 1923 vintage.** T.B. Owen Courtesy Colour-Rail

Following the introduction of unpainted aluminium R Stock on the District Line, the earlier red-painted cars were repainted silver. This colour was later changed to white, as seen on car 23425 by the fruit stall on Earl's Court station. Capital Transport

The CO/CP Stock was moved to the District from the Circle and Hammersmith Lines by the introduction of the new C69 Stock. The new stock programme enabled the replacement of the remainder of the Q Stock by more batches of CO/CP Stock. The last Q Stock train ran on the District on 30th June 1971. In 1977 more C Stock was introduced, known as the C77 Stock, which began to take over the Edgware Road to Wimbledon service from April 1978. The C Stock is based on the Hammersmith Depot of the Circle and Hammersmith Line but is worked by District crews for District services.

The improvements to services and facilities on the District were appreciated by everyday passengers and the more famous. In August 1969, the Rt Hon Harold Macmillan, former Prime Minister, was spotted travelling on the District, remarking that it was the best way to 'get from A to B'. In 1973, Marlene Dietrich, playing at the Wimbledon Theatre but staying in central London, travelled daily on the District Line, finding it much quicker than road transport, a fact still valid today. Sixteen years later, a District Line timetable was one of the 1980-era objects buried by Michael Heseltine in a time capsule in the foundation stone of a building at Millbank.

**A train of C69 Stock at Whitechapel.**
Capital Transport

**As C Stock is also used on the Circle Line, where increased standing room and quick boarding and alighting are particularly important, the trains have four sets of double doors per car.**
Capital Transport

By the time the C Stock was entering service on the Edgware Road branch, the programme was well in hand for the replacement of the whole of the District Line fleet. The first of the new trains, known as the D78 Stock, entered service in January 1980. It was from this time onwards that the District main line fleet could at last be of one type of train.

Following experience gained with the 1973 Tube Stock built for the Piccadilly Line, it was found possible to design a 6-car train for the District Line which had the same capacity as a 7-car train using cars of about 60ft in length, about 8ft longer than the traditional District Line car. The vehicle width also had to be reduced by about 4 inches to allow the dimensions to remain within the District Line loading gauge on some of the sharp curves.

**A train of D stock at Southfields on the Wimbledon branch.** P.M. Bradley

Following the introduction of its new rolling stock in the early 1980s, the District also participated in the programme of station modernisation on the Underground in general. Mansion House and Monument have been two of the beneficiaries. Capital Transport

On the new trains, it was decided to use four 3ft 6in door openings per car with 48 seats for those without cabs and 44 seats for those with cabs. A narrower than normal door width was chosen to allow a single leaf door to be used. This allowed the amount of door operating equipment to be considerably reduced. Increases in traffic since the late 1970s when the stock was designed have shown that a wider door opening would be more beneficial.

Although passenger door operation had been tried on the Underground during the 1950s and 1960s, it was not a great success because in those days the public was less used to such systems. However, in response to repeated requests from passengers to find ways of retaining heat in cars during the colder weather, it was decided to try passenger door operation again. This time the system proved much more successful and is now a standard feature on all new trains to be used by London Underground.

The introduction of rolling stock with door controls in the drivers' cabs eventually allowed the introduction of One Person Operation (OPO). This was introduced without the need to install the expensive automatic train operation equipment used on the Victoria Line but required the installation of cameras, screens and mirrors suitably positioned on platforms to enable drivers to monitor the station stops and assure him of passengers' safety when operating the doors. Train radio has also been fitted to give rapid communication with the line controller. The Circle Line was converted to OPO in 1984 and the District Line followed in 1985.

Following the new fire safety standards introduced by London Underground, it has been decided that all rolling stock should be refurbished with a higher standard of fire resistant materials than currently fitted. At the same time the opportunity will be taken to paint the unpainted aluminium body to overcome the effects of graffiti. As the District Line has one of the most modern fleets on the Underground, the programme for the D Stock has been deferred until older stocks in worse condition have been completed. Nevertheless it is hoped that work on this will begin within the next few years to provide passengers with a fleet which has the best that can be achieved in modern safety and aesthetic standards. At the same time it is planned to undertake a series of engineering modifications to improve the reliability of the stock. In the meantime, the District Line has benefited from the appearance of refurbished C Stock in the programme for the Circle and Hammersmith Lines, stock also used on the Wimbledon and Olympia branches.

In the longer term, the District Line's Wimbledon branch may form part of a planned new line from Wimbledon to north east London via Chelsea, central London and Hackney. Ownership of the section between East Putney and Wimbledon was transferred from British Rail to London Underground in April 1994. Despite loss of route mileage over the years — such as that to South Harrow and to Hounslow now served by the Piccadilly — the District remains the Underground line with the most stations, covering 40 miles of the system with its fleet of 75 trains.

Opposite **As part of the District Line's 125th anniversary celebrations in 1993, steam trains operated in passenger service — for those buying special tickets — between Ealing Broadway and West Kensington on the first weekend of June. One of these trains is seen at Ealing Common.** Mike Esau

**Part of the District Line's heritage: West Brompton station retains many of its original features.**
Capital Transport

Overleaf
**Gloucester Road platforms, refurbished in 1993 with cleaned-up original brickwork.**
Taylor Woodrow